HOME
where life makes up its mind...

Charles R. Swindoll

Foreword by
Howard G. Hendricks

MULTNOMAH PRESS

Other Multnomah Press books by Charles R. Swindoll:

FOR THOSE WHO HURT
SECOND WIND: A FRESH RUN AT LIFE
KILLING GIANTS, PULLING THORNS

PHOTOGRAPHY BY: Dewitt Jones
DESIGN BY: Dannelle Pfeiffer

FIRST PRINTING, 1979
Copyright©1979 by MULTNOMAH PRESS, Portland, Oregon 97266

Printed in the United States of America

ISBN: 0-930014-31-6 paper

0-930014-32-4 cloth

Library of Congress Cataloging in Publication Data

Swindoll, Charles R.
    Home, where life makes up its mind.

    1. Family--Religious life. I. Title.
BV4526.2.S77   248:.4   79-90363
ISBN 0-930014-32-4
ISBN 0-930014-31-6 pbk.

Foreword

Society seems to be telling us that life is a circus. If we were to judge from media commentators, America's merry-go-round is in full swing. Lights flash, melodies lilt, and mirrors reflect gyrating riders on wooden horses and painted ponies. Home is a plastic drive-in where listless transients grab a cheap meal and change their blue jeans.

Home—if we hear Chuck Swindoll—does indeed sparkle, radiate, and exhilarate. But the riders mounted on real life race to an eternal destiny. Home is the seed plot for the unfictitious family drama, the kernel from which bona fide kids grow. Chuck writes with the easy familiarity of one on well-trodden turf. He and Cynthia have for two decades been my friends, students, and fellow-learners in the lessons of family life. I am not surprised that he reaches into the helter-skelter of living and holds out ready-to-use couplings to bind homes and families together.

I commend his keen eye to every young mother and father in our land. His is a sane word of encouragement. Godly young families can flourish in our world—and they will!

Howard G. Hendricks
Professor of Christian Education
Dallas Theological Seminary

HOME

Whatever else may be said about home, it is the bottom line of life, the anvil upon which attitudes and convictions are hammered out. It is the place where life's bills come due, the single most influential force in our earthly existence. No price tag can adequately reflect its value. No gauge can measure its ultimate influence . . . for good or ill. It is at home, among family members, that we come to terms with circumstances. It is here life makes up its mind.

Words cannot declare how highly I treasure my home . . . each member of my family. Those who live under the same roof with me stimulate and fulfill the deepest longings of my life. Except for my personal relationship with Jesus Christ, I know of nothing that brings more satisfaction than time spent with my wife Cynthia and our four children: Curt, Charissa, Colleen, and Chuck. The love, purpose, joy, peace, and understanding I glean from our home defies description. Since all six of us are in the process of growing and learning, very few things stay the same around our place. And since it's "life in the fast lane" rather than a rocking chair on the back porch, we often move along at a pretty fast clip.

But that doesn't mean we're always on the run. It isn't uncommon for us to spend time discussing issues that are important. In the give-and-take of discussion and disagreement, we are continually filing away at the rough edges of ideas, shaping and molding our minds together. When we come to those hard questions that cannot be answered one, two, three—you know, like a formula—we'll probe deeply into the what and when, asking why and how. Such times are stretching, requiring an enormous amount of acceptance and tolerance to pull it off. But in the Swindoll family, we place a high premium on mutual respect and self-esteem. We believe that without those ingredients a lot of stuff floats around without handles, breeding confusion, fear, and insecurity. And those three words describe a lot of homes today— maybe even yours.

I care about that! In fact, that's why I have written this book. Perhaps you will gain a little insight or learn a technique or two that will help. You might even sense a new surge of encouragement, at least I hope so.

I've tried to capture a few vignettes from our home life much like a bug on our ceiling might observe. The last thing you should imagine is that ours is the perfect family that has it all together. Just like you and yours, we are imperfect, occasionally frustrated and irritable, even failing and wondering if we will ever model the message we say we believe. Every now and then some dust will settle and things that once were up for grabs appear to be taking shape. And as that piece of the puzzle falls into place, as that part of life makes up its mind, it is reassuring and so satisfying.

It might help you to know I've spent about eight years putting these thoughts and experiences into print. Many of these chapters first appeared in a column I wrote in our church's weekly newsletter. As a member of the pastoral team in this dynamic local church, the First Evangelical Free Church of Fullerton, California, I am allowed the time and freedom to use my pen as well as my voice in ministry. Would that every pastor could be as fortunate to have such an encouraging and appreciative congregation as I! To them, as well as to Helen Peters, my secretary who typed these words, and to Larry Libby of Multnomah Press who edited the manuscript, I openly express my gratitude.

But most of all, my highest tribute is directed to the mother of our four, my irreplaceable wife, who said "I do" on June 18, 1955, having no idea what in the world she was getting into. Hopefully, the satisfaction she receives from reading these pages will be a sufficient ransom to restrain her from revealing all the things she has had to endure and overlook from this author.

If she ever tells it all, I'm finished.

Charles R. Swindoll
Fullerton, California

Backing Off

*K*ids are nutty.

Some friends of ours in Texas have two little girls. The younger child is constantly on the move, rarely winding down by bedtime. So the nightly affair has become something of a familiar routine. A story from her favorite book. A drink of water. A prayer. A song. Her doll. Another drink of water. A kiss. A hug. A third sip of water. A trip to the bathroom. A warning. Another kiss. You know, the whole bit.

One night her dad decided he'd be Mr. Nice Guy, the epitome of patience and tolerance. He did it all. Not once did he lose his cool. When Miss Busybody finally ran out of requests, her daddy slipped out of the room, heaved a sigh of relief, and slumped into his favorite chair by the fireplace. But before he could stretch out and relax, there was a piercing scream from the jitterbug's room. Startled, he dashed down the hall and rushed to her bedside. Great tears were rolling down the little girl's face.

"What's wrong? What happened?"

"I burnt my tongue."

Baffled, he tried again. "You what?"

"I burnt my *tongue!*" she yelled.

"How in the world did you do that?" he asked.

"I licked my night-light."

That really happened. She couldn't control her curiosity. She simply had to discover how it would feel to lick that little thing that glowed so warmly and serenely by her bed. Rude was her awakening to the fact that lights are strictly for lighting . . . not licking. And tongues are made for tasting . . . not testing. You and I realize that the best thing our little friend could have done was to stay in bed, keep her tongue to herself, and allow the light to fulfill its appointed function. But she didn't—and she got burned.

In the book of Ecclesiastes, Solomon, the wise, passes along to us a list of various types of "appointed times" on earth. Among them he mentions:

> . . . *a time to heal . . . a time to shun embracing*
> *. . . a time to give up as lost . . . a time to be silent . . .*

I see in these words of counsel one strong undercurrent of advice: BACK OFF! It is often wise to relax our intensity, refuse to force an issue, allow nature to take its course, "let sleeping dogs lie." Backing off, says Solomon, provides opportunity for healing to occur, opportunity for perspective to break through the storm clouds of emotion and illuminate a difficult situation with a fresh understanding.

When the time is right, things flow very naturally, very freely. To rush or force creates friction-scars that take years to erase. Intensity leads to futility. Like the little boy who plants the seed and then nervously digs it up every day to see if it is growing. Waiting is as necessary as planting and fertilizing.

When the fish aren't biting, banging on the water with an oar won't help. You can't get sap out of a hoe handle. Nor can a relationship be corrected by legislation and force. Remember, God says there is a "time to shun embracing" just as there are times to embrace. "Giving up as lost" may, on some occasions, be the wisest response, though extremely painful. Sometimes that means simply being silent and allowing God to work. In other words, *back off* so God can move in. This is never more essential than among family members in a home. Allowing some loose slack in the rope is, at the right time, a mark of real wisdom.

What a difficult pill for up-tight parents to swallow! Kept edgy by impatience, rigidity, and unbending determination, they foolishly rush in where angels loathe to tread. The result? Exasperated kids. Rooms choked with threats and irritating pressure.

Young guys can do this with girls they date. She wants room to

breathe, some space to think things out for herself, but he continues to smother. We can do this with people we have offended. They need time to reason, freedom to forgive without being hurried. To push for a quick closure is like a hard-sell salesman pressing you to buy when you are trying to decide what's best. The faster he talks and the harder he pushes, the less interested you become in buying. Even something you *need.* The wise salesman knows when to allow you the privilege of deciding for yourself— when to back off and leave you alone.

Nobody is able to eat while they're weeping. Serving more food isn't the answer. The appetite will return when the agony subsides . . . and not until. That takes time.

Stop and think. Think first about your family. Then your other friends. Are you being wise or foolish? Are you using force or providing freedom? Are you being pushy or patient? Are you intimidating by your intensity . . . or backing off and relaxing? Are you allowing the ground fog to roll back or are you launching blindly into dangerous flight?

Take it from one who has learned this difficult lesson the hard way—keep a tight bridle on your tongue, relax and settle for a good night's sleep. Otherwise, you're going to get pushy, you're going to get caught with your tongue in the wrong place . . . and you're going to get burned.

Relaying the Truth

It was late afternoon when the boat's engine sputtered, stalled, and refused to restart. Gallons of water surged into the craft as it pitched on sickening, six-foot swells. The five Jaegers had done all they knew to do, but it wasn't enough. An exciting fishing trip was now a thing of horror. They were going under.

Grim-faced, George Jaeger, his three sons, and his elderly father methodically tightened the buckles on their life jackets, tied themselves together with a rope, and slipped silently into a black and boiling Atlantic.

George glanced at his watch as the boat finally disappeared—6:30 p.m. Very little was said. It grew dark. First one boy and then another swallowed too much saltwater, gagged and strangled on the brine as they fought to keep their heads up. The helpless father heard his sons, one by one, and then his dad choke and drown. But George couldn't surrender. After eight nightmarish hours, he staggered onto the shore, still pulling the rope that bound him to the bodies of the other four. Pause and try to imagine the sight!

"I realized they were all dead—my three boys and my father—but I guess I didn't want to accept it, so I kept swimming all night long," he later told reporters. "My youngest boy, Clifford, was the first to go. I had always taught our children not to fear death because it was being with Jesus Christ." Before Cliff died, his dad heard him say, "I'd rather be with Jesus than go on fighting."

In that vivid Atlantic memory, George Jaeger had a chance to witness the impact of his 15 years as a father. The boys died quietly, with courage and dignity. Up to the very last minute, one by one they modeled the truth passed on by their father: When under pressure, stay

12

calm . . . think . . . even if death is near, keep under control. So they did and so they died. When the ultimate test was administered in an angry sea, they handed in perfect scores.[1]

In her bestseller, *What Is a Family?*, Edith Schaeffer devotes her longest chapter to the idea that a family is a *perpetual relay of truth.*[2] A place where principles are hammered and honed on the anvil of every-day living. Where character traits are sculptured under the watchful eyes of moms and dads. Where steel-strong fibers are woven into the fabric of inner constitution.

The relay place. A race with a hundred batons.

- *Determination.* "Stick with it, regardless."
- *Honesty.* "Speak and live the truth—always."
- *Responsibility.* "Be dependable, be trustworthy."
- *Thoughtfulness.* "Think of others before yourself."
- *Confidentiality.* "Don't tell secrets. Seal your lips."
- *Punctuality.* "Be on time."
- *Self-control.* "When under stress, stay calm."
- *Patience.* "Fight irritability. Be willing to wait."
- *Purity..* Reject anything that lowers your standards."
- *Compassion.* "When another hurts, feel it with him."
- *Diligence.* "Work hard. Tough it out."

And how is this done? Over the long haul, believe me. This race is not a sprint, it's a marathon. There are no 50-yard dash courses on character building. Relays require right timing and smooth hand-offs—practiced around the track hour after hour when nobody is look-ing. And where is this practice track? Where is this place where rough edges cannot remain hidden, must not be left untouched? Inside your own front door. *The home* is God's built-in training facility.

That's why He urged all the dads in Moses' day to relay the truth:

. . . and you shall teach them diligently to your sons and shall talk of them when you sit in your house and when you walk by the way and when you lie down and when you rise up (Deuteronomy 6:7).

That's the plan—the inimitable strategy which makes winners out of runners. Relay the truth—diligently, consistently. One final warning, however. If you determine to make this your goal, you'll have to out-distance two relentless foes: slow starts and sloppy handoffs. Keep in mind, moms and dads, you really don't have forever. Negligence will catch you from behind and beat you in the stretch if you let up. And don't think your kids will let you get away with faking it, either.

I just read about a salesman who knocked on the door of a rundown apartment house in a low-rent district. The mother didn't want to talk to the guy, so she told her little boy to tell him she couldn't come to the door because she was in the bathtub. Her son answered the door this way: "We ain't got no bathtub, but Mom told me to tell you she's in it."[3]

Furthermore, it won't work for you to play catch-up by dumping a truckload of truth once or twice a year. The secret of good parenting is consistency. Never forget that.

Got the game plan, now? Stay at it, day in and day out. And make sure your handoffs are crisp and sharp throughout this race against time. Relays are won or lost at that critical moment when a young hand reaches back and gropes for the baton.

Ask George Jaeger.

The Winsome Witness

$\mathcal{T}$onight was fun 'n' games night around the supper table in our house. It was wild. First of all, one of the kids snickered during the prayer (which isn't that unusual) and that tipped the first domino. Then a humorous incident from school was shared and the event (as well as how it was told) triggered havoc around the table. That was the beginning of 20 to 30 minutes of the loudest, silliest, most enjoyable laughter you can imagine. At one point I watched my oldest literally fall off his chair in hysterics, my youngest doubled over in his chair as his face wound up in his plate with corn chips stuck to his cheeks . . . and my two girls leaning back, lost and preoccupied in the most beautiful and beneficial therapy God ever granted humanity: *laughter.*

What is so amazing is that everything seemed far less serious and heavy. Irritability and impatience were ignored like unwanted guests. For example, during the meal little Chuck spilled his drink twice . . . and even *that* brought the house down. If I remember correctly, that made six times during the day he accidentally spilled his drink, but nobody bothered to count.

All is quiet now, a rather unusual phenomenon around here. It's almost midnight and although my bones are weary, I'm filled and thrilled with the most pleasant memories a father can enjoy—a healthy, happy, laughing family. What a treasure! The load that often weighs heavily upon my shoulders about this time each week seems light and insignificant now. Laughter, the needed friend, has paid another dividend.

If you ask me, I think it is often just as sacred to laugh as it is to pray . . . or preach . . . or witness. But then—laughter *is* a witness in many ways. We have been misled by a twisted, unbalanced mind if we have come to think of laughter and fun as being carnal or even questionable. This is one of Satan's sharpest darts and from the looks and long lines on our faces, some of us have been punctured too many times. Pathetic indeed is the stern, somber Christian who has developed the look of an old basset hound through long hours of practice in restraining humor and squelching laughs.

Looking stern and severe is nothing new. The frowning fraternity of the sour set got started in the first century. Its charter members were a scowling band of religious stuffed shirts called Pharisees. I hardly need to remind you that Jesus' strongest words were directed at them. Their super-serious, ritually rigid life style nauseated our Lord. This brings me to a related point of contention I have with artists who portray Jesus Christ perpetually somber, often depressed. You simply cannot convince me that during 33 years as a carpenter and discipler of the Twelve He never enjoyed a long, side-splitting laugh. Wouldn't it be refreshing to see a few pictures of Jesus leaning back with His companions, thoroughly enjoying a few minutes of fun with them? Surely that isn't heresy!

Picture in your mind Martin Luther, the reformer. What do you see? A stern-faced, steel-jawed, frowning fighter with his German fist clenched and raised against wrong? *Wrong!*

Several of his biographers inform us that he *abounded* in an unguarded, transparent sincerity . . . plain and pleasant honesty . . . playful humor and mirth. Small wonder he attracted the oppressed, browbeaten people of his day like flies to honey. The reformer, you see, wasn't afraid to laugh. In one word, surprising though it may seem, Luther was *winsome.*

Let's try another famous name: Charles Haddon Spurgeon, the great preacher of London. What do you see? A sober, stoop-shouldered pastor who dragged the weight of sinful England around with a rope? Try again!

Spurgeon was a character. His style was so loose he was criticized again and again for bordering on frivolity in the Tabernacle pulpit. Certain incensed fellow clergymen railed against his habit of introducing humor into his sermons. With a twinkle in his eye, he once replied:

"If only you knew how much I hold back, you would commend me."

. . . .

"This preacher thinks it less a crime to cause a momentary laughter than a half-hour of profound slumber."[4]

Spurgeon dearly loved life. His favorite sound was laughter—and frequently he leaned back in the pulpit and *roared aloud* over something that struck him funny. He infected people with cheer germs. Those who caught the disease found their load lighter and their Christianity brighter. Like Luther, Spurgeon was *winsome.*

Winsomeness. That tasteful, appealing, ultra-magnetic quality . . . that charisma . . . that ability to cause joy and genuine pleasure in the thick of it all. When a teacher has it, students line up for the course. When a dentist or physician has it, his practice stays full. When a salesman has it, he gets writer's cramp filling out orders. When an usher has it, the church is considered friendly. When a college president has it, the public relations department has a downhill slide. When a coach has it, the team shows it. When a restaurant owner has it, the public knows it. When parents have it, kids grow it.

Winsomeness *motivates.* It releases the strangle-hold grip of the daily grind. It takes the sting out of reality. Winsomeness *simplifies.* Things suddenly become less complicated . . . less severe . . . less bothersome. The hole at the end of the tunnel becomes far more significant than the dark passage leading to it. Winsomeness *encourages.* Without ignoring the wrong, winsomeness focuses on the benefits, the hope, the answers. Even when it must deal with jagged disappointment or inescapable negatives, winsomeness stands tall and refuses to spend the night in such dwellings.

Winsome humor is an asset beyond value in the life of a missionary. Indeed, it is a most serious deficiency if a missionary lacks the ability to find something to smile about in diverse and difficult situations. I recently read of a Swede who was urged by friends to give up the idea of returning to India as a missionary because it was so hot there. "Man,"

17

he was exhorted, "it's 120 degrees in the shade!" "Vell," countered the Swede in noble contempt "ve don't always have to stay in the shade, do ve?"[5]

Some frowning, neurotic soul is reading this and saying, "Well, somebody's got to do the job. Life is more than a merry-go-round. Laughter is all right for schoolgirls—but adults, especially *Christian adults,* have a task to perform that's deadly serious." Okay, pal, so it's serious. So it isn't all a joke. Nobody's going to argue that life has its demands and that being mature involves discipline and responsibility. But who says we have to get an ulcer and drive ourselves (and each other) to distraction in the process of fulfilling our God-given role? No one is less efficient or more incompetent than the person on the brink of a breakdown, who has stopped having fun, who is nursing a bleeding ulcer, who has become a pawn in the brutal hands of relentless respon-sibilities, who has begun a one-man crusade for *whatever,* who has lost the ability to relax and laugh and "blow it" without guilt. Our hospitals are full—literally jammed—with the victims of the let's-cut-the-fun philosophy of life. And today, quite frankly, they really aren't much of an asset to society—nor to the cause of Christ. That is not a criticism—it's reality.

By a sense of humor, I am neither referring to distasteful, inap-propriate, vulgar jesting, nor foolish and silly talk that is ill-timed, of-fensive, and tactless. I mean that necessary ingredient of wit—en-joyable, delightful expressions or thoughts—which lifts our spirits and lightens our day.

How is such winsomeness cultivated—and communicated—in our homes and among our other contacts? What practical steps can be taken to yank us out of the doldrums? I suggest three specific projects:

1. Start each day with pleasant words. Your family will be the first to benefit (better have the glycerin tablets ready). No need to dance around like Bozo the clown or force jokes into your sleepy mate's ears. Just be pleasant in your remarks, cheerful with your greetings. As you are slipping out of bed, thank God for His love . . . His calm, fresh reminders that this new day is under His control. Quietly state the en-

couraging truth: God loves me.

2. Smile more often. I cannot think of many occasions when a smile is out of place. Develop a cheerful countenance. A frowning face repels. A smile reaches out and attracts. God gave you this gift that radiates encouragement. Don't fence it in . . . loosen up, break that concrete mask—*smile.* You might even release a laugh or two this month if you want to get fanatical about it.

3. Express at least one honest comment of appreciation or encouraging remark to each person you are with during the day. As a Christian, you want to share Christ's love. You want to lift up hearts that are heavy. Spot strengths—and say so. Steadfastly decline to camp on others' weaknesses. Ask the Lord to make you genuinely interested in others instead of so occupied with yourself. Ask Him to enable you to take the risk and reach out. Ask Him to be winsome through you.

In spite of bleak and serious surroundings about us, I firmly believe we need another good dose of Solomon's counsel. Listen to David's wisest son:

A joyful heart makes a cheerful face, but when the heart is sad, the spirit is broken . . . all the days of the afflicted are sad, but a cheerful heart has a continual feast (Proverbs 15:13, 15).

A joyful heart is good medicine (the Hebrew says, ". . . causes good healing . . .") *but a broken spirit dries up the bones* (Proverbs 17:22).

Honestly now . . . how's your sense of humor? Are the times in which we live beginning to tell on you—your attitude, your face, your outlook? If you aren't sure, ask those who live under your roof, they'll tell you! Solomon talks straight, too. He (under the Holy Spirit's direction) says that three things will occur in the lives of those who have lost their capacity to enjoy life: (1) a broken spirit, (2) a lack of inner healing, and (3) dried-up bones. What a barren portrait of the believer!

Have you begun to shrivel into a bitter, impatient, critical Christian? Is your family starting to resemble employees at a local mortuary? The Lord points to a better way—the way of joyful winsomeness. "A joyful heart" is what we need . . . and if ever we needed it, it is now.

The Law of Echoes

A young boy lived with his grandfather on the top of a mountain in the Swiss Alps. Often, just to hear the sound of his own voice echoing back to him, he would go outside, cup his hands around his mouth and shout, "HELLO!" Up from the canyons the reply reverberated, "HELLO . . .HELLO . . . hello . . . hello . . ." Then he would call out, " I LOVE YOU . . . I LOVE YOU . . . I love you . . . love you . . . love you. . . ."

One day the boy seriously misbehaved and his grandfather disciplined him severely. Reacting violently, the child shook his fist and screamed, "I HATE YOU!" To his surprise, the rocks and boulders across the mountainside responded in kind: " I HATE YOU . . . I HATE YOU . . . I hate you . . . hate you . . . hate you . . ."

And so it is in a family. We could call it one of the immutable laws of physical nature. More particularly, *human nature.* We get in return exactly what we give. It all comes back. Incredible echoes mirror our actions to an emphatic degree, sometimes in greater measure than we give. The results are often embarrassing . . . or tragic.

What was it Jesus once said? Luke tells us:

Treat men exactly as you like them to treat you . . . . Don't judge other people and you will not be judged yourselves. Don't condemn and you will not be condemned. Make allowances for others and people will make allowances for you. Give and men will give to you . . . For whatever measure you use with other people they will use in their dealings with you (Luke 6:31, 37-38 Phillips).

Let's call it the law of echoes. Tennyson said:

Our echoes roll from soul to soul and grow forever and forever.[6]

21

The law of echoes applies to a marriage. You want a wife who is gracious, forgiving, tolerant, and supportive? Start with her husband! It will roll from your soul to hers, my friend. As our Savior put it, "Treat her exactly as you would like her to treat you." That's quite a promise. But it rests on quite an assignment.

The law of echoes applies to our work as well. The rocky canyons within the lives of others are ready to echo back the identical attitudes and actions we initiate. Want your associates at work to be cheery and unselfish, free from catty, caustic comments and ugly glares? The place to begin is with that person who glares back at you from the bathroom mirror every morning.

The law is remarkably consistent. Children echo their parents; pupils in a classroom are usually echoes of teachers; a congregation of worshipers is more often than not a reflection of the pastor. If the one communicating is negative, severe, blunt, and demanding . . . guess what? The echo reflects those same characteristics, almost without exception.

I read recently about a teacher who asked a group of students to jot down, in 30 seconds, the names of the people they really disliked. Some of the students could think of only one person during that half minute. Others listed as many as 14. The interesting fact that emerged from the research was—*those who disliked the largest number of people were themselves the most widely disliked.*

The law of echoes. If you want others to judge and condemn you, you start it. If you want them to be understanding, broad-minded, allowing you room to be you—then begin by being that way yourself. Like begets like. Smiles breed smiles. A positive attitude is as contagious as Hong Kong flu. Unfortunately, so are frowns, sighs, and harsh, abrasive words. Whatever you deposit in the echo bank, you draw in return. Sometimes *with interest.*

A missionary was sitting at her second story window when she was handed a letter from home. As she opened the letter, a crisp, new, ten-dollar bill fell out. She was pleasantly surprised, but as she read the letter her eyes were distracted by the movement of a shabbily dressed stranger down below, leaning against a post in front of the building. She couldn't get him off her mind. Thinking that he might be in greater financial stress than she, she slipped the bill into an envelope on which she quicky penned "Don't despair." She threw it out the window. The stranger below picked it up, read it, looked up, and smiled as he tipped his hat and went his way.

The next day she was about to leave the house when a knock came at the door. She found the same shabbily dressed man smiling a toothless grin as he handed her a roll of bills. When she asked what they were for, he replied:

"That's the 60 bucks you got comin', lady. *Don't Despair* paid five to one."[7]

Building Memories

*Y*ou guys go on without me. You'll have a great time—I'm sure of that. Sorry, family, but I have to work."

The place? Montgomery, Alabama.

The time? Several years ago.

The situation? A dad, who really loved his family and wanted them to enjoy a summer vacation, had to work. The press of business kept him tied to the office. But being committed to their happiness, he assured them of his desire that they take the trip and enjoy the fleeting summer days.

He helped them plan every day of the camping trip. They would load up the family station wagon, drive to California, camp up and down the coast, then travel back home together. Each day was carefully arranged—even the highways they would travel and the places they would stop. Dad knew their whole route, the time they would reach each state—planned almost to the hour—even when they would cross the Great Divide.

It's what he didn't tell them that made the difference.

The father took off work (he'd planned it all along) and arranged to have himself flown to an airport near where his family would be on that particular day of the trip. He had also arranged to have someone pick him up and drive him to a place where every car on that route had to pass. With a wide grin, he sat on his sleeping bag and waited for the arrival of that familiar station wagon packed full of kids and camping gear. When he spotted the station wagon, he stood up, stepped out onto the shoulder of the road, and stuck out his thumb.

Can you visualize it?

24

"Look! That guy looks just like . . . DAD!"

The family assumed he was a thousand miles away, sweating over a stack of papers. It's amazing they didn't drive off into a ditch or collapse from heart failure. Can you imagine the fun they had the rest of the way? And the memories they stored away in their mental scrapbook—could they ever be forgotten?

When later asked by a friend why he would go to all that trouble, the unusually creative father replied, "Well . . . someday I'm going to be dead. When that happens, I want my kids and my wife to say, 'You know, Dad was a lot of fun.' "[8]

Talk about a unique domestic game plan! What an outstanding model of a father who wants to be remembered for more than just the basics—the bare essentials . . .

> *". . . turn out the lights."*
> *"Did you get that bed made?"*
> *"Get out there and cut the grass."*
> *"No, we can't. I gotta work."*
> *"How much does it cost?"*
> *"That's too much trouble, dear. Let's be practical."*
> *"Hold it down—I can't hear the news."*

Oh—but there's so much more in life! The beautiful music of living is composed, practiced, and perfected in the harmony of home. The freedom to laugh long and loudly . . . the encouragement to participate in creative activities . . . the spontaneity of relaxed relationships that plant memories and deepen our roots in the rich, rare soil of authentic happiness. Couldn't this be included in the "all things" Paul mentioned in Romans 8:32 and 1 Timothy 6:17? The apostle tells us that our God *"richly supplies us with all things to enjoy."*

We're missing it—God's best—if the fun memories are being eclipsed by the fierce ones. The world outside the family circle is dark enough. When the light goes out *within* the circle . . . how great is the darkness.

If life with mom and dad has become more of an endurance course than a refreshing catalyst, then your prime time project isn't too tough to identify. Too many of us are beginning to resemble stern-faced East

German guards patrolling the wall rather than approachable, believable parents, building happy memories. And maybe even a few crazy ones, too. Don't worry, God can handle it. He's got a great sense of humor. He made *you,* didn't He?

I'd much rather my brood remember me as the dad who tossed their mother fully clothed into the swimming pool—and lived to tell the story—than the preacher who frowned too much, yelled too loud, talked too long . . . and died too young.

Traveling

B. J. Thomas sings my kind of tune when he strums the chords to "Home Where I Belong." You can tell the guy's been on the road a lot when he punches out lines like:

When I'm feelin' lonely and when I'm feelin' blue,
It's such a joy to know that I am only passin' through.
I'm headed home, I'm goin' home, where I belong.[9]

The plain and simple truth is: Be it ever so humble, there's no place like it. No place! Never will be. No scene any more beautiful than one step inside the front door. Anybody who loves his family and treasures time around the supper table followed by a couple hours arm-in-arm in front of a warm fireplace with his gang will quickly testify that being gone on a trip— no matter how significant—is much more a drag than a dream.

Funny thing, to the person who doesn't travel much, zinging across the country appears super-glamorous and exciting. Swept up, up, and away, cradled in the glistening arms of an L-1011, flashing across the sky at breakneck speed to some distant destination, the traveler seems the envy of all his peers. Especially those whose responsibilities and demands clip their wings and cage them from such ecstatic, exotic episodes. Face it, how could *anyone* imagine that grinding it out in traffic, with the kids, under the pile day in and day out—how could *anyone* even think of comparing that to those carefree jaunts travelers enjoy? Just listen to the jingles . . . "Get away from it all . . . " "Fly our friendly skies . . ." "We're ready when you are . . ." "Doing what we do best . . ." Sure sounds better than the consequences connected with having so much lead in your pants that the only time you can get away is when you hide in the closet with an arm load of diapers, mumbling stuff like, "This too shall pass . . ." and "Help me make it through the day."

While all that may be true, believe me, there's another side of traveling that never gets much press. Like being bumped to standby because they overbooked your flight . . . and then arriving at the hotel only to discover they gave your room to another party because you didn't get there before six o'clock. Like having your luggage go on to Berlin for the week and you're caught in a March blizzard in Toronto with only sneakers and a sweater . . . and you gotta borrow some shaving gear from the guy next door whose face is broken out with terminal acne. Like being stuck on an elevator between floors 14 and 12 with an older woman who was taking her two nervous poodles out for their evening break . . . and she tends to faint in close places. Like being served a toadstool omelet for breakfast then spending the next two days cramped up in the fetal position, wondering if your will is in order and how the wife and kids are going to get along without you. Like aniticipating a nice relief in your schedule only to discover you're expected to speak 14 times in 3 days—plus an all-day seminar with 200 discouraged pastors and several depressed couples whose marriages are on the rocks. And the TV doesn't work—so you miss the final NCAA championship basketball game that evening. And you run out of clean shorts. And you step on your glasses getting out of the shower. And you're driven to the airport by a guy who grins a lot and says "Praise the Lord" 41 times. And you come back to Los Angeles on a 5-hour flight in a jam-packed 727, holding a box of Pampers for the mother of twins who have colic. And one just kicked your coffee over. And your briefcase handle pulls loose. And your in-box at the office looks like the Leaning Tower. And the first five people you see the next day ask cutely, "Well—how was the vacation?"

Hold it! Let it be once-and-for-all understood that every bowl of cherries has its pits. That there ain't no such thing as a free lunch. That all those airline and travelogue commercials are dreamed up by the same fiction writers who did the scripts to *Star Wars* and *Superman* and *The*

Wizard of Oz. And they moonlight for *Mad Comics.* And finally, until further notice, let it be indelibly written in every mind that if there is any way on earth you can *keep* from traveling, do it!

I am more amazed than ever that the apostle Paul voluntarily took those three long journeys across thousands of miles back in Century One. And that he operated so effectively out of a backpack and a sleeping bag, eating who knows what and staying who knows where. For months, sometimes years! That's beyond me! But there is one thing, I *do* understand. When it says he hurried on occasion to get back home, that's no longer a mystery to me. Everybody has his limit. A guy can take just so much punishment . . . whether it's a powerful preacher named Paul or a singing Texan named Thomas or a lonesome, homesick Californian named Chuck, who's tired of breathing air he can't see and sleeping in places without his wife and kids.

Where I belong is home.

Acting Medium

The children worked long and hard on their own little cardboard shack. It was to be a special spot—a clubhouse—where they could meet in solemn assembly or just laugh, play games, and fool around. As they thought long and hard about their rules, they came up with three rather perceptive ones:

1. *Nobody act big.*
2. *Nobody act small.*
3. *Everybody act medium.*[10]

Not bad theology!

In different words, God says the very same thing:

. . . give preference to one another in honor (Romans 12:10).

. . . through love serve one another (Galatians 5:13).

. . . whoever wishes to become great among you shall be your servant, and whoever wishes to be first among you shall be your slave (Matthew 20:26-27).

Let another praise you, and not your own mouth; a stranger, and not your own lips (Proverbs 27:2).

Just "act medium." Believable, honest, human, thoughtful, and down-to-earth. Regardless of your elevated position or high pile of honors or row of degrees or endless list of achievements, just stay real. Work hard at counteracting the celebrity syndrome. Junk any idea that you deserve some kind of pat on the back or engraved wristwatch for a job well done. Who did you do it for, anyway? If you did it for God, He has an infinite number of unseen ways to reward you. If you did it for man, no wonder you're clawing for glory! But it's so subtle. So easy to draw out that praise for yourself, isn't it? Especially around the house when you do a few extras.

A certain firm has made headlines out of deflating overblown egos. Its well-trained employees accept contracts to squash juicy pies into the faces of various pompous individuals. In its first few months, over 60 hits were made at $35 per splash! All on disbelieving, immaculately dressed, prim-and-proper victims.

Imagine this scene: A dignified, well-tailored executive vice-president waits for the elevator to open on the 18th floor. As he steps out, a stranger whips a pie out of a cardboard box and splosh! Giving the pie a professional twist, the hit-man jumps into the elevator headed for the main floor. There stands Vice President Shmotz . . . his once-spotless suit, matching vest and tie now dripping with lemon meringue goo and crust.

An employee of the pie-tossing company said, "A pie in the face brings a man's dignity down to where it should be and puts the big guys on the same level with everyone else."[11]

Even Biola College weathered the recent pie-throwing rage. No one was safe from the meringue gang—neither the professors nor even the school's great hearted president who took it on the chin like a champ. I'd hate to think how many college presidents would have responded with their superguarded, highly polished egos smeared with bright gold pumpkin pie and whipping cream. In about two and a half seconds, the whole school would know the truth, the whole truth, and nothing but the truth. I wonder how many profs would "act medium."

Again what was it the son of David said?

Let another praise you . . . a stranger, and not your own lips.

Meaning what? Meaning no self-reference to some enviable accomplishment. Meaning no desire to manipulate and manufacture praise. Meaning authentic surprise when applauded. Genuine, rare humility—regardless.

Like the inimitable Principal Cairns, headmaster of an English school, who was walking onto the platform in a line of dignitaries. As he stepped up, a burst of spontaneous applause arose from the au-

dience as an expression of their appreciation. In characteristic modesty, Cairns stepped back to let the man behind pass by as he began to applaud his colleague. He genuinely assumed the applause was for another.[12]

One final warning. Don't try to fake it. False humility smells worse than raw conceit. The answer lies not in trying to appear worthless and wormy. Folks in your family won't fall for that. Rather, be sensitive to the achievements, skills, and contributions of others. And say so. That's one way to serve others in love. Like Christ.

Got the rules memorized? They're really not that difficult. "Nobody act big. Nobody act small. Everybody act medium." Wise counsel from a cardboard clubhouse whose membership is pretty good at practicing what it preaches.

And they also laugh out loud when you get a pie in the kisser. Believe me, I know.

The Cure for Tunnel Vision

The splinter in my thumb this morning brings back pleasant memories of yesterday's diversion. Cranking up the old radial-arm saw in my garage, I wound up with two pecky cedar window box planters. I plunged into the project with the zeal of a paratrooper, ecstatic over the airborne sawdust, delighting over every angle, every nail, every hammer blow, even the feel of the wood and the scream of the saw. I caught myself thinking about nothing but the next cut and its proper measurement . . . the exhilaration of accomplishment . . . the sheer joy of doing something totally opposite of my career and completely different from my calling. Periodically, I looked up through the sawdust and prayed, "Lord, I sure do like doing this!" In this terror-filled aspirin age, my saw and I gave each other wide, toothy grins.

It was Sir William Osler, the Canadian-born physician and distinguished professor of medicine at Johns Hopkins University, who once told an audience of medical men:

> *No man is really happy or safe without a hobby, and it makes precious little difference what the outside interest may be—botany, beetles or butterflies; roses, tulips or irises; fishing, mountaineering or antiques—anything will do as long as he straddles a hobby and rides it hard.*[13]

A worthier prescription was never penned. Diversions are as essential to our health and personal development as schools are to our education, or as food is to our nourishment. And it's funny—you can always tell when it's time to shift gears and change hats. The frown gets deeper . . . the inner spirit gets irritable . . . the jaw gets set . . . the mind gets fatigued—these are God's signals to you that say, "Don't abort, divert. Don't cave in, get away! Don't crumble, create!" The

35

saddest believers I know—those most bored, most lonely, most miserable, most filled with self-pity—are those who have never developed interests outside the realm of their work.

The only vision they possess is *tunnel vision,* the most significant thing they've ever created is an *ulcer,* the only thing they can discuss in depth is their old nine-to-five routine. No thanks! That's not a career, it's a sentence. It may be fulfilling the demands of an occupation, but you'll never convince me it's the experience of "abundant life" our Lord Jesus talked about.

Ladies and girls, sit down this very evening and read Proverbs 31:10-31. This passage describes a woman of great worth—a valuable human being. The interesting thing to note is that she has such balance. She is *not* locked into the dull demands of a routine existence. She is notably efficient in several areas *outside* the home and *beyond* the church.

Men, give attention to such characters as Nehemiah or Job (when he was healthy) or David or Paul. Mark these names down on the ledger of guys who recognized the value and joy of involvement and accomplishment outside the boundaries of their "stated" occupations. One used his hands in construction, another composed music, another raised cattle.

Before you shelve this discussion, I challenge you to answer these four questions:

Can you name at least one area of interest (outside the limits of your "calling") which you are presently developing?

Do you experience as much satisfaction in your diversion as you do in your occupation (sometimes more!)?

Whenever you plunge into your diversion, is it without guilt and without anxiety?

Are you aware that your diversion is as significant to God and to your own happiness as your actual vocation?

If your answer to any of the above is "No," you need a few splinters in your thumb. They may help you forget the worries in your head.

TRESPASS
FEE-DAY USE
NO CAMPING
$1.00-PER PERSON

No FIRES

Ghirardelli
MILK CHOCOLATE
with MACADAMIA
NUTS

Grace Revisited

*M*ost of us did not learn to pray in church.

And we weren't taught it in school, or even in pajamas beside our bed at night. If the truth were known, we've done more praying around the kitchen table than anywhere else on earth. From our earliest years we've been programmed: If you don't pray, you don't eat. It started with Pablum in the high chair, and it continues through porterhouse at the restaurant. Right? Like passing the salt or doing the dishes, a meal is incomplete without it.

Our first impressions of communicating with the Almighty were formed in the high chair with cereal and pudding smeared all over our faces. We peeked and gurgled while everybody else sat silent and still. We then learned to fold our hands and close our eyes. Soon we picked up the cue to add our own "Amen" (which usually followed ". . . in Jesus' name"). Then came the day we soloed. We mumbled, looked around, got mixed up, then quickly closed with a relieved "Amen!" as we searched Mom and Dad's faces for approval.

Then we went through three very definite stages over the next eight to ten years of grace—stages that are common in most Christian families. Stage one . . . *snickering.* For some strange reason, prayer before the meal became the "comedy hour" when I was growing up. In spite of parental frowns and glares, threats and thrashings . . . my sister and I could *not* keep from laughing. I remember one time we giggled so long and so loud that our mother finally joined in. My older brother was praying (he usually remembered every missionary from Alaska to Zurich) and purposely refused to quit. He finished by praying for the *three of us.*

Stage two . . . *doubting.* This is a cynical cycle, a tough one to endure. We start questioning the habit—the custom. With an air of pseudo-sophistication, we think:

"What does it matter if I *don't* say grace?

"This is a ritual—it serves no purpose—God knows I'm grateful."

Junior high years abound with these maverick thoughts. The whole scene of bowing heads and closing eyes and saying "religious words" suddenly seems childish . . . needless.

Stage three. . . *preaching.* This one is difficult to handle because it usually comes from well-meaning lips. Out of sincerity and a desire to prompt obedience, we use the time in prayer as an avenue to rebuke a family member or (very subtly) reinforce our own piety. Parents can easily fall into this manipulative technique, since it's impossible to be interrupted in prayer. The temptations of taking to the platform before our captive audience seems irresistible.

After passing through these stages, however, we begin to realize how good it is to cultivate this healthy habit. "Asking the blessing" is a sweet, much-needed, refreshing pause during hectic days. But since it occurs so often, the easiest trap to fall into is sameness. The perfunctory uttering of meaningless, repetitious cliches that become boring *even to God!* Our Lord Jesus thundered warning after warning against the empty verbosity which characterized the Pharisees.

Without claiming to have all the answers, I offer several suggestions a family can build on together.

1. *Think before you pray.* What's on the table? Call the food and drink by name. "Thank you, Lord, for the hot chicken-and-rice casserole in front of us. Thanks for the cold lemonade . . ." What kind of day are you facing—or have you faced? Pray with those things in mind. Draw your prayer out of real life. Don't lapse into mechanical mutterings or convenient religious jargon. You're not just "saying a blessing," you're talking to your God!

2. *Involve others in prayer.* Try some sentence prayers around the table. Ask the family for requests.

3. *Sing your table blessing.* Try it a few times. After the family has recovered from the shock of shattering the norm, it might catch on.

39

The Doxology, a familiar hymn, or a chorus of worship works great . . . and offers a change of pace. Holding hands can be meaningful.

4. *Keep it brief, please.* There's nothing like watching a thick film form over the gravy while you plow through all five stanzas of Wesley's "And Can It Be?" Remember what the blessing is all about—a pause to praise our faithful Provider—a moment of focus on the Giver of every good gift. You don't have to pray around the world three times or highlight every relative between the poles and all the ships at sea. God's watching the heart, not totaling up the verbiage.

5. *Occasionally pray after the meal.* When the mood is loose or the meal is served in "shifts" or picnic-style settings, be flexible. An attitude of worship is occasionally much easier when the hunger pangs have eased up.

Is your prayer time at the table losing its punch? Here's a way to find out. When the meal is over and you get up to do the dishes, ask if anyone remembers what was prayed for. If they do, great. If they don't, sit back down at the table and ask why. You've got a lot more to be concerned about than a stack of dishes.

Lifelines

*T*oday I just turned 45.

No big deal . . . just another stabbing realization that I'm not getting any younger. I know that because the cake won't hold all the candles. Even if it could, the frosting would melt before I'd be able to blow all of them out. My kind and thoughtful secretary suggested another approach. She gave me a birthday card depicting a wizened old codger tottering beside a cake *covered* with candles. On the front it reads:

Don't feel you're getting old if you can't blow out all the candles . . .

and inside:

. . . just beat 'em out with your cane.

If I was hoping for comfort and encouragement from my children . . . I shouldn't have. In all seriousness my youngest asked me recently if they had *catsup* when I was a boy. I tried not to look offended—he could have asked if they had the *wheel.* But I took pains to inform him that we not only had catsup . . . but also electricity, talking movies, the radio, cars, and indoor plumbing. He gave me that you-gotta-be-kidding look and walked out of the room shaking his head. I suddenly felt the need to lie down and take a nap.

But birthdays are milestones. Significant points in the passing of time. Specific yet mute reminders that more and more sand has passed through our hour glass. They do, however, give us a handle on the measurement of time which, when you boil it down into minutes, gets up and *moves.* There are 60 of them every hour . . . 1440 every day . . . over 10,000 of them each week . . . about 525,000 per year. As of today—I've experienced over 23 million of them. Talk about feeling old!

But they pass so quietly, so unobtrusively, so consistently they fool you. That's part of the reason C. S. Lewis used to say:

The safest road to Hell is the gradual one—the gentle slope, soft underfoot, without sudden turnings, without milestones, without signposts. [14]

The long, dull, monotonous years of middle-aged prosperity or middle-aged adversity are excellent campaigning weather [for the devil]. [15]

We mark our calendars with *deadlines*—dates that set limits for the completion of objectives and projects. To ignore these deadlines brings consequences. To live without deadlines is to live an inefficient, disorganized life, drifting with the breeze of impulse on the fickle wave of moods. We set deadlines because they help us accomplish the essentials; they discipline our use of time; they measure the length of our leash on the clothesline of demands.

God, however, brings about birthdays . . . not as deadlines but *lifelines.* He builds them into our calendar once every year to enable us to make an annual appraisal, not only of our length of life but also our depth. Not simply to tell us we're growing older, but to help us determine if we are also growing deeper.

These lifelines are not like that insurance policy you invested in several years ago. There's no automatic promise of annual renewal. Obviously, if God has given you another year to live for Him, He has some things in mind, some very special plans to pull off through your life. Surely it includes more than existing 1,440 minutes a day!

It's been awhile since you've slowed down enough to take stock of where you are going, hasn't it? And how about an evaluation of the kids? Or your marriage? Or the direction your family is heading. Or your own future? You know what I mean. Trimming off the fat of lazy thinking and taking a lean, hard look at the years remaining. If Christ doesn't return (and I don't die in the meantime), I figure I've got about 20 to 25 remaining years of effective service. How old are you? Stop and figure how many years lie between now and when you turn 65 or 70 years of age. See what I mean?

If that doesn't grab you, consider your family in the next decade. In

only ten years my wife Cynthia and I will have a son 28 years old, a daughter 26, another daughter 22, and our "baby" will be 19! It's possible that none of our brood will be living at home . . . in only ten short years. Seems impossible. Especially since our place today resembles a cross between the Indianapolis 500, O'Hare Airport, and the San Diego Zoo.

How we need those lifeline days for regrouping and evaluation! Even the sports world has its time out, seventh-inning stretch, pit stop and half time, so why shouldn't we? Before the smoke from your birthday candles blends into the humdrum atmosphere of the day after, force yourself to pull off the road. Ask yourself some hard questions. Here are a few worth personal consideration:

1. Am I really happy, genuinely challenged and fulfilled in life?

2. In light of eternity, am I making any consistent investment for God's glory and His cause?

3. Is the direction of my life currently leading me toward a satisfying and meaningful future?

4. Can I honestly say that I am in the nucleus of God's will for me?

And how about the kids?

1. Am I spending sufficient time with my children? Do they have a firm grasp on the fact that I love them, accept them, and care very much about their future? Am I consistent in my discipline . . . maintaining the standards?

2. Am I communicating life goals, a proper value system, a model of moral purity, a drive for excellence, and commitment to loyalty, integrity, generosity, and honesty to my children? Do they really *know* how I feel about these things?

3. When they leave the nest, will they be able to stand alone?

What are you asking the Lord for on behalf of your life and children? I challenge you, stop long enough to think it over. But don't just think, get alone and *write down* your thoughts, your dreams, your aspirations. Refuse to let tonight's television programs or some insignificant activity interrupt this necessary discipline. Don't wait for your birthday. In God's economy, *today* is of the utmost importance.

HOME IS A LOT OF THINGS . . . BUT MAINLY
IT IS THE PLACE WHERE LIFE MAKES UP ITS MIND.[16]

The psalmist gives us the perfect prayer to pray every year our lifeline rolls around.

Teach us to number our days aright, that we may gain a heart of wisdom (Psalm 90:12 NIV).

Good advice! Socrates put it another way:

The life which is unexamined is not worth living.[17]

Now let me caution you. Don't expect wisdom to come into your life like great chunks of rock on a conveyor belt. It isn't like that. It isn't splashy and bold . . . nor is it dispensed like a prescription across a counter. Wisdom comes privately from God as a by-product of right decisions, godly reactions, and the application of scriptural principles to daily circumstances. Not from trying to do great things for God, but from being faithful in the small, obscure tasks few people ever see.

Are you just growing *old*. . . or are you also growing *up*? As you "number your days," do you just count years--the grinding measurement of minutes--or can you find marks of wisdom, character traits that were not there when you were younger?

Take a look. You really don't have a lot longer, you know. As a matter of fact, one of these years, your lifeline will be God's deadline.

Tough Days

*Y*ou've heard them. Those all-too-familiar cries of exasperation. Maybe a couple have crossed *your* mind today sometime between the too-early clang of the alarm and the too-late racket of the neighbors next door.

Going from bad to worse.

Jumping from the frying pan into the fire.

Between a rock and a hard place.

He said, "Cheer up, things could get worse," So I cheered up—and sure enough, things got worse!

My mother told me there would be days like these, but she never said they would run in packs.

Tough days. We all have them. Some are worse than others. Like the one the hard-hat employee reported when he tried to be helpful. Maybe you heard about it too; the account actually appeared on a company accident form. Bruised and bandaged, the workman related this experience:

When I got to the building I found that the hurricane had knocked off some bricks around the top. So I rigged up a beam with a pulley at the top of the building and hoisted up a couple barrels full of bricks. When I had fixed the damaged area, there were a lot of bricks left over. Then I went to the bottom and began releasing the line. Unfortunately, the barrel of bricks was much heavier than I was—and before I knew what was happening the barrel started coming down, jerking me up.

I decided to hang on since I was too far off the ground by then to jump, and halfway up I met the barrel of bricks coming down fast. I received a hard blow on my shoulder. I then continued to the top, banging my head

47

against the beam and getting my fingers pinched and jammed in the pulley. When the barrel hit the ground hard, it burst its bottom, allowing the bricks to spill out.

I was now heavier than the barrel. So I started down again at high speed. Halfway down I met the barrel coming up fast and received severe injuries to my shins. When I hit the ground, I landed on the pile of spilled bricks, getting several painful cuts and deep bruises. At this point I must have lost my presence of mind, because I let go of my grip on the line. The barrel came down fast—giving me another blow on my head and putting me in the hospital.

I respectfully request sick leave.

Yeah, I would imagine!

Some days you honestly wonder why you ever crawled out from under the covers that morning . . . and later, if you will ever make it back to bed that night. Most of us have little difficulty fielding a couple or three problems during the day, but when they start coming down like hail, with no relief, rhyme, or reason, we get jumpy. More often than not we also get grumpy. Invariably there are those who love us and really want to help. But, try all they like, tough days are usually solo flights. Others only complicate matters.

Take the four guys who decided to go mountain climbing one weekend. In the middle of the climb, one fella slipped over a cliff, dropped about 60 feet and landed with a thud on the ledge below. The other three, hoping to rescue him, yelled, "Joe, are you okay?"

"I'm alive . . . but I think I broke both my arms!"

"We'll toss a rope down to you and pull you up. Just lie still!" said the three.

"Fine," answered Joe.

A couple of minutes after dropping one end of the rope, they started tugging and grunting together, working feverishly to pull their wounded companion to safety. When they had him about three-fourths of the way up, they suddenly remembered he said he had broken *both* of his arms.

48

"Joe! If you broke both your arms, how in the world are you hanging on?"

Joe responded, "With my TEEEEEEEEEEETH . . . ."

No, other people can't help much on tough days. They may be good companions, but they sure can't stop the pain. Holding hands and singing during an earthquake is small comfort.

Some would advise, "Just get in there and keep busy—work harder." But that doesn't help much either. When the barn's on fire, slapping a coat of paint on the other side doesn't make much sense. If the tires are flat, driving faster is pretty dumb.

So—what's the answer? How can we handle tough days when the enemy works overtime to persuade us that God doesn't care? Just recently, I have found solid encouragement from four threads woven into the fabric of Galatians 6. See if you don't agree.

1. *Let us not lose heart* (verse 9). On tough days, you gotta have heart. Don't quit, whatever you do. Persevere. Stand firm. Be strong, resilient, determined to see it through. Ask God to build a protective shield around your heart, stabilizing you.

2. *Let us do good* (verse 10). Our tendency will be anything but that. Instead of good, we will feel like doing evil. Fume. Swear. Scream. Fight. Pout. Get irritated. Burn up all kinds of emotional BTU's. Rather than parading through that shopworn routine, stay quiet and consciously turn it *all* over to the Lord.

3. *Let no one cause you trouble* (verse 17). Superb advice! Refuse to allow anyone (or any*thing*) to gain mastery over you. That throne within you belongs only to the Lord Jesus Christ. Stop leasing it out!

4. *Let grace be with your spirit* (verse 18). Allow the full impact of grace to flow through your thoughts, your attitudes, your responses, your words. Open the gates and let those good things stampede freely across your tough day. You sit on the fence and relax.

It works. It *really* does. Even at home.

Even on sick leave.

A Rabbit on the Swim Team

The Springfield, Oregon, Public Schools Newsletter published an article that caught my eye some time ago. As I read it, it struck me that I was reading a parable of a familiar frustration in the Christian home and the Body of Christ today.

Once upon a time, the animals decided they should do something meaningful to meet the problems of the new world. So they organized a school.

They adopted an activity curriculum of running, climbing, swimming and flying. To make it easier to administer the curriculum, all the animals took all the subjects.

The duck *was excellent in swimming; in fact, better than his instructor. But he made only passing grades in flying, and was very poor in running. Since he was slow in running, he had to drop swimming and stay after school to practice running. This caused his web feet to be badly worn, so that he was only average in swimming. But average was quite acceptable, so nobody worried about that—except the duck.*

The rabbit *started at the top of his class in running, but developed a nervous twitch in his leg muscles because of so much make-up work in swimming.*

The squirrel *was excellent in climbing, but he encountered constant frustration in flying class because his teacher made him start from the ground up instead of from the treetop down. He developed "charlie horses" from overexertion, and so only got a C in climbing and a D in running.*

The eagle *was a problem child and was severely disciplined for being a non-conformist. In climbing classes he beat all the others to the top of the tree, but insisted on using his own way to get there . . . .*[18]

The obvious moral of that story is a simple one—each creature has its own set of capabilities in which it will naturally excel—unless it is expected or forced to fill a mold that doesn't fit. When that happens, frustration, discouragement, and even guilt bring overall mediocrity or complete defeat. A duck is a duck—and *only* a duck. It is built to swim, not to run or fly and certainly not to climb. A squirrel is a squirrel—and *only* that. To move it out of its forte, climbing, and then expect it to swim or fly will drive a squirrel nuts. Eagles are beautiful creatures in the air but not in a foot race. The rabbit will win every time unless, of course, the eagle gets hungry.

What is true of creatures in the forest is true of Christians in the family; both the family of believers and the family under your roof. God has not made us all the same. He never intended to. It was He who planned and designed the differences, unique capabilities, and variations in the Body. So concerned was He that we realize this, He spelled it out several times in His final will and testament. Please take the time to read the 32 verses of 1 Corinthians 12 *slowly* and *aloud.*

Let's summarize some of these compelling truths:

God has placed you in his family and given you a certain mixture that makes you unique. No mixture is insignificant!

That mix pleases Him completely. Nobody else is exactly like you. That should bring you pleasure, too.

When you operate in the realm of capabilities, you will excel, the whole Body will benefit, and you will experience incredible satisfaction.

When others operate in their realm, balance, unity, and health automatically occur in the Body. But when you compare . . . or force . . . or entertain expectations that are beyond your or others' God-given capabilities, mediocrity or frustration or phoniness or total defeat is predictable.

If God made you a duck saint—you're a duck, friend. Swim like mad, but don't get bent out of shape because you wobble when you run or flap instead of fly. Furthermore, if you're an eagle saint, stop expecting squirrel saints to soar, or rabbit saints to build the same kind of nests you do.

52   I'll let you in on my own experience—the trap I fell into years ago. Having

been exposed to a few of the "greats" in various churches and an outstanding seminary, I (like some of the other guys in the class) tried to be like *them.* You know, think like, sound like, look like. For over ten years in ministry I—a rabbit—worked hard at swimming like a duck or flying like an eagle. I was a frustrated composite creature . . . like that weird beast in the second chapter of Daniel. And my feet of clay were slowly crumbling beneath me. It was awful! The worst part of all, what little bit of originality or creativity I had was being consumed in that false role I was forcing. One day my insightful and caring wife asked me, "Why not just be *you*? Why try to be like anybody else?" Well, friends and neighbors, this rabbit quit the swim team and gave up flying lessons and stopped trying to climb. Talk about relief! And best of all, I learned it was okay to be me . . . and let my family members be themselves. Originality and creativity flowed anew!

So relax. Enjoy your spiritual species. Cultivate your own capabilities. Your own style. Appreciate the members of your family or your fellowship for who they are, even though their outlook or style may be miles different from yours. Rabbits don't fly. Eagles don't swim. Ducks look funny trying to climb. Squirrels don't have feathers.

Stop comparing. There's plenty of room in the forest.

Restraint

*Y*esterday I got drunk.

Now wait a minute! Before you pick up your phone and notify six of your closest friends, let me explain. I was the victim of a dentist's drill. As he was about to do his thing on my ivories, he inserted 80 milligrams of *Nembutol* into my innocent bloodstream . . . resulting thereafter in a flow of words and actions that were *anything* but innocent, I am told. I have been informed that a tape recording was made which probably would call into question my ordination as well as cause my old Marine Corps drill instructor to blush. I am sure that the entire dental office—that group of rascals!—has sufficient information to blackmail me. But they are sworn to secrecy. I hope.

My neighbors probably raised some eyebrows when my dear wife helped me out of the car and I staggered to the door, singing loudly. She informed me that I saw a mosquito and took a rather exaggerated swing at it. That led to a few other verbal expressions totally unlike a man of the cloth. When I awoke on the patio three hours later, my children were still giggling and snickering over my irresponsible homecoming. They also are sworn to secrecy. *They better be!*

Isn't it amazing what happens when the clamps of restraint are loosened? In some cases it's unbelievable! I would never, under normal conditions, declare: *"Dentistry is a rip-off!"* But I did yesterday. Right in front of my dentist and his drill team. I would not say to a young lady, *"You talk too much— get out!"* But that's exactly what I said to one of his capable assistants.

Thanks to *Nembutol,* I became an open book with no secret sections or hidden chapters containing guarded, private feelings and thoughts. For several unrestrained hours, my emotions ran rampant, and there's no way to recover the damage or remove the raw facts from that page of my life.

Of course, I was under the influence of a pain-killing drug, so I'm automatically excused, or so they assure me. Because of the circumstances, it's nothing more than a funny, harmless episode that makes us chuckle.

But that isn't always so.

The removal of restraint is usually neither excusable nor amusing. In fact, restraining ourselves is so important that God lists it as a fruit of the Spirit in Galatians 5:22-23. *Self-control,* another word for restraint, is honored by the Lord as the "anchor virtue" on His relay team that runs life's race for His glory. Many other voices are saying, "Let it all hang out" and "tell it like it is" and "hold nothing back" and "be open . . . express your feelings without restraint!" It's easy to buy that kind of advice. But when I go to my Bible, I find contrary counsel being marketed.

When we are angered, God instructs us to restrain ourselves. For proof, ponder Proverbs 14:29, 15:1, and 29:11, along with Ephesians 4:26-27. He further tells us not even to associate with one given to anger (Proverbs 22: 24-25) or place him into leadership in the church (1 Timothy 3:2-3).

When we are tempted, He admonishes us to say "No" to lust and restrain our carnal nature (1 Corinthians 9:26-27; 2 Timothy 2:22).

When we are prompted to talk too much, He says, "Hold it! Better keep that to yourself!" (Proverbs 17:28; Job 13:5; Ephesians 4:29). Restraint of the tongue is a mark of wisdom. It is a slippery eel in need of being in check between our cheeks.

When food is stacked before us, God is pleased when we restrain ourselves from gluttony (Proverbs 23:1-2; 1 Corinthians 10:31-32). Being fat is a tell-tale sign that control is lacking.

When money is to be earned, spent, saved, or invested, the use of restraint is the order of the day (Matthew 6:19-21; Luke 14:28-30; Romans 13:7-8).

Removing restraint from your life may seem like an exciting adven-

55

ture, but it inevitably leads to tragedy. It's a lot like removing the brakes from your car. That may be daring and filled with thrills for awhile, but injury is certain. Take away the brakes and your life, like your car, is transformed into an unguided missile—destined for disaster.

Let's all learn a lesson from my extra-curricular escapades this week.

When medicine is needed
To dull the pain you're in,
Your actions may be silly
Yet they really are not "sin."

But when you willfully lose control
And set restraint aside
Your actions then are sinful
And pain is multiplied.

The Lonely Hitchhiker

*E*verybody says they want it, but most people run right by it.

Contentment is the lonely hitchhiker back somewhere in the rearview mirror as the transfixed driver hurdles by on the expressway. Few bother to notice they've sped past the very thing they kept saying they were looking for. And even if they did notice a blurred object in their peripheral vision, there was really no time to slow down and investigate. Went by too fast. And the traffic moves on.

Books on contentment decorate the windows of a thousand bookstores. And keep right on selling. Isn't it strange that we need a book to help us experience what ought to come naturally? No, not really. Not when you've been programmed to compete, achieve, increase, fight, and worry your way up the so-called "ladder of success" (which few can even define). Not when you've worshiped at the shrine of PROMOTION since infancy. Not when you've served all your life as a galley slave on the ship of *Public Opinion*. To you, contentment is the unknown "X" in life's equation. It is as strange to you as living in an igloo or raising a rhinoceros in your backyard.

Face it. You and I are afraid that if we open the door of contentment, two belligerent guests will rush in—loss of prestige and laziness. We really believe that "getting to the top" is worth *any* sacrifice. To proud Americans, contentment is something to be enjoyed between birth and kindergarten, retirement and the rest home, or (and this will hurt), among "those who have no ambition."

Stop and think. A young man with keen mechanical skills and little interest in academics is often counseled against being contented to settle for a trade right out of high school. A teacher who is competent, contented, and fulfilled in the classroom is frowned upon if she turns down an offer to become principal. The owner of *El Taco Loco* on the corner has a packed-

58

out joint everyday—and is happy in his soul, contented in his spirit. But chances are selfish ambition won't let him rest until he opens ten other places and gets rich—leaving contentment in the lower drawer of forgotten dreams. A man who serves as an assistant . . . or any support personnel in a ministry, company, or the military . . . frequently wrestles with feelings of discontent until he or she is promoted to the top rung of the scale—regardless of personal capabilities.

Illustrations are legion. This applies to mothers and homemakers or nuclear scientists...plumbers or cops...engineers or seminary students...caretakers or carpet layers...artists or waitresses. This riduculous pattern would be hilarious if it weren't so tragic...and common. Small wonder so many get frostbitten amidst the winter of their discontent.

"Striving to better, oft we mar what's well," wrote ye olde Shakespeare.[19] It's a curious fact that when people are free to do as they please, they usually imitate each other. I seriously fear we are rapidly becoming a nation of discontented, incompetent marionettes, dangling from strings manipulated by the same, dictatorial puppeteer.

Listen to Jesus: *"...be content with your wages"* (Luke 3:14b).

Hear Paul: *"I am well content with weaknesses...if we have food and covering...be content!"* (2 Corinthians 12:10, 1 Timothy 6:8).

And another apostle: *"...let your life be free...being content with what you have"* (Hebrews 13:5).

Now I warn you—this isn't easy to implement. You'll be outnumbered and outvoted. You'll have to fight the urge to conform. Even the greatest of all apostles admitted, "I have learned to be content" (Philippians 4:11). It's a learning process, often quite painful. And it isn't very enjoyable marching out of step until you are convinced you are listening to the right drummer.

When you are fully convinced, two things will happen: (1) Your strings will be cut, and (2) you'll be free, indeed! And funny thing: You'll find that lonely hitchhiker you left miles back sitting in the passenger seat right beside you... smiling every mile of the way.

Dialogues of the Deaf

It is impossible to overemphasize the immense need humans have to be really listened to, to be taken seriously, to be understood. No one can develop freely in this world and find a full life without feeling understood by at least one person . . .

Listen to all the conversations of our world, between nations as well as those between couples. They are for the most part dialogues of the deaf.[20]

So wrote Dr. Paul Tournier, the eminent Swiss psychiatrist and author. His words convict me. They usually do . . . but *these* especially. Because they probe at an area of weakness in my own life. Not a glaring weakness; a subtle one. One that I'm able to hide from most folks because I'm often the one who's expected to talk. But some time ago it began to dawn on me that I needed to cultivate a discipline far more difficult than talking . . . and one that required an exceptional amount of skill.

Listening.

I don't mean just hearing. Not simply smiling and nodding while somebody's mouth is moving. Not merely staying quiet until it's "your turn" to say something. All of us are good at that game—cultivated in the grocery store, local laundromat, or on the front steps of the church building. You know, skating across that cold, superficial layer of ice summarized so well in the lyrics of Paul Simon's *Sounds of Silence.*

And in the naked light I saw
Ten thousand people, maybe more,
People talking without speaking,
People hearing without listening

60

People writing songs that voices never shared.
No one dared
Disturb the sounds of silence.[21]

Dialogues of the deaf! Sounds come from voice boxes; guttural noises are shaped into words by tongues and lips. But so little is listened to—I mean *really* taken in. As Samuel Butler once stated:

It takes two people to say a thing—a sayer and a sayee. The one is just as essential to any true saying as the other.[22]

Illustration: *Children.* They express their feelings. Deep down in their fragile, inner wells are a multitude of needs, questions, hurts, and longings. Like a tiny bucket, their tongues splash out these things. The busy, insensitive, preoccupied parent, steamrolling through the day, misses many a cue and sails right past choice moments never to be repeated or retrieved.

Or how about the person we spot without Christ? Have you ever practiced *listening evangelism?* Unless we're careful we usually unload the goods and go for the scalp. But people bruise easily. Sometimes irreparably. We must take care not to fold, spindle, mutilate, or assault! Sure, the gospel must ultimately be shared, but taking the time to listen patiently and respond calmly is an essential part of the process. I nodded with agreement when I read the admonishment of a rough and ready tycoon as he began the meeting with: "Now listen slowly!"

Check out Christ with the woman at the well (John 4). He could have blown her away with an endless barrage of verbal artillery. He didn't. He genuinely listened when she spoke; he "listened slowly." He read the lines of anxiety on her face and felt the weight of guilt in her heart. As she talked,He peered deeply into the well of her soul. It wasn't long before she found herself completely open, yet not once did she feel forced or needlessly embarrassed. His secret? He listened. He studied every word, each expression. Even the tone of her voice.

What does it take? Several things. Rare qualities. Like caring. Time. Unselfishness. Concentration. Holding the other person in high

61

esteem. Sensitivity. Tolerance. Patience. Self-control. And—perhaps most of all— allowing room for silence while the other person is thinking and trying to get the words out. Wise is the listener who doesn't feel compelled to fill up all the blank spaces with verbiage.

Solomon said it clearly in Proverbs 20:12:

The hearing ear and the seeing eye,
The Lord has made both of them.

Two ears. Two eyes. Only one mouth. Maybe that should tell us something. I challenge you to join me in becoming a better listener. With your mate. Your friend. Your kids. Your boss. Your teacher. Your pupils. Your clients. Your fellow Christians as well as those who need to meet Christ.

If those who battle with blindness need Seeing Eye dogs, we can be certain that those who struggle through dialogues of the deaf need Hearing Ear friends.

The Tailor's Name is Change

*W*hen you boil life down to the nubbies, the name of the game is *change.* Those who flex with the times refuse to be rigid, resist the mold, and reject the rut—ah, *those* are the souls distinctively used by God. To them, change is a challenge, a fresh breeze that flows through the room of routine and blows away the stale air of sameness.

Stimulating and invigorating as change may be—it is never easy. Before you get all jazzed about some quick and easy change you plan to carry out, better read that sentence again, pal. Changes are especially tough when it comes to certain habits that haunt and harm us. That kind of change is excruciating—but it isn't impossible.

Jeremiah pointed out the difficulty of breaking into an established life pattern when he quipped:

> *Can the Ethiopian change his skin*
> *or the leopard its spots?*
> *Neither can you do good*
> *who are accustomed to doing evil* (13:23 NIV).

Notice the last few words, "accustomed to doing evil." The Hebrew says, literally, "learned in evil." Now that's quite an admission! We who are "learned in evil" cannot do good; evil habits that remain unchanged prohibit it. Evil is a habit that is learned; it is contracted and cultivated by long hours of practice. In another place, Jeremiah confirms this fact:

> *I warned you when you felt secure,*
> *but you said, "I will not listen!"*
> *This has been your way from your youth;*
> *you have not obeyed me* (22:21 NIV).

All of us have practiced certain areas of wrong from our youth. It is a pattern of life that comes "second nature" to us. We gloss over our resistance, however, with the varnish of excuse:

"Well, nobody's perfect."
"I'll never be any different; that's just the way I am."
"I was born this way—nothing can be done about it.'
"You can't teach an old dog new tricks."

Jeremiah tells us why such excuses come so easily. We have become "learned in evil" . . . it has been our way from our youth. In one sense, we have learned to act and react in sinful, unbiblical ways with *ease* and (dare we admit it?) with a measure of *pleasure.* Admittedly, there are many times we do it unconsciously; and, on those occasions, the depth of our habit is more revealing.

It is vital—*it is essential*—that we see ourselves as we really are in the light of God's written Word . . . then be open to change where change is needed. I warn you, the number one enemy of change is the hard-core, self-satisfied sin nature within you. Like a spoiled child, it has been gratified and indulged for years, so it will not give up without a violent temper tantrum. Change is its *greatest* threat, and a confrontation between the two is inevitable. Change must be allowed to face and conquer the intimidations of inward habit—and I repeat the warning that a nose-to-nose meeting will never be an easy one.

The flesh dies a slow, bitter, bloody death—kicking and struggling all the way down. "Putting off" the clothes of the old man (the old, habitual life style) will not be complete until you are determined to "put on" the garment of the new man (the new, fresh, Christian life style). The tailor's name is Change, and he is a master at fitting your frame. But the process will be painful . . . and costly.

Change—real change—takes place slowly. In first gear, not overdrive. Far too many Christians get discouraged and give up. Like ice skating or mastering a musical instrument or learning to water ski, certain techniques have to be discovered and developed in the daily discipline of living. Breaking habit patterns you established during the passing of *years* cannot occur in a few brief days. Remember that. "Instant" change is as rare as it is phony.

God did not give us His Word to satisfy our curiosity; He gave it to change our lives. Can you name a couple of specific changes God has implemented in your life during the past six or eight months? Has He been allowed, for example, to change your attitude toward someone . . . or an area of stubbornness . . . or a deep-seated habit that has hurt your home and hindered your relationship with others for a long, long time . . . or a pattern of discourtesy in your driving . . . or a profane tongue . . . or cheating . . . or laziness?

Perhaps a better question would be, "Exactly what changes do you have on your personal drawing board?"—or—"What are you asking the Lord to alter and adjust in your life that needs immediate attention?"

The tailor's real name is the Holy Spirit. You can count on Him to dispose of your old threadbare wardrobe as quickly as He outfits you with the new. By the way, He's also on call 24 hours a day when you have the urge to slip into the old duds "just one more time." If you ask Him, He'll help you remember what you looked like on the day you first walked into His shop. His has a mirror with memories—the Bible.

'Nuff said.

Gentleness

"Tough and tender."[23]

That's the way my friend Joyce Landorf describes what every woman wants in a man. Her plea is for a balanced blend, an essential mixture of strong stability *plus* consideration, tact, understanding, and compassion. A better word is *gentleness*. But for some peculiar reason, that idea seems alien to the masculine temperament.

Observe the media-myth man. The man portrayed on the tube is rugged, hairy, built like a linebacker, drives a slick sports car, and walks with a swagger. In the beer ads he's all out for grabbing the gusto. With women he is a conqueror . . . fast and furious. In business he's "bullish." Even with a razor or hair dryer he's cocky, superconfident. If you don't believe it, *ask him*. The media-myth is, basically, *tough*. Spanish-speaking people would say he is known for his *machismo*. To the majority of young men—that's their hero, their masculine model.

Now let's understand something. A man *ought* to be a man! Few things are more repulsive than a man who carries himself like a woman . . . or wears stuff that suggests femininity. And we are living in an era when the roles are definitely eroding. I heard about a preacher who was conducting a wedding ceremony for a couple like this—both bride and groom having the same length hair and dressed in similar attire. Confused over their identity, he closed the ceremony with:

Would one of you kiss the bride?

The right kind of toughness—strength of character—ought to mark the man of today . . . but not only that. Tenderness—gentleness—is equally important.

67

God considers it so important He places it on the list of nine qualities He feels should mark the life of His children:

But the fruit of the Spirit is love, joy, peace, patience, kindness, goodness, faithfulness, gentleness, self-control; against such things there is no law (Galatians 5:22-23).

There it is . . . number eight. The Greek word translated "gentleness" is *Prautes,* and it brims with meaning. In secular writings, the Greeks used it when referring to people or things that demonstrated a certain soothing quality—like an ointment that took the sting out of a burn. They also used this word to describe the right atmosphere which should prevail during a question-answer period in a classroom; the idea of discussing things without losing one's temper or becoming strongly defensive.

And think about this one. *Prautes* described the controlled conduct of one who had the power to act otherwise. Like a king who chose to be gracious instead of a tyrant. Like a military commander who patiently trained an awkward squad of soldiers. Plato called *Prautes* "the cement of society" as he used this word in the sense of politeness, courtesy, and kindness.

Gentleness has *three close traveling companions* in the New Testament:

1. It keeps company with agape-love (1 Corinthians 4:21).
2. It is a friend of meekness (2 Corinthians 10:1).
3. It is attached to humility (Ephesians 4:2).

Similarly, according to the New Testament, gentleness is the proper attitude when faced with *three difficult assignments:*

1. When faced with the need to exercise discipline in the Body of Christ (Galatians 6:1).
2. When faced with personal opposition (2 Timothy 2:25).
3. When faced with the truth of God's Word—being open and teachable (James 1:21).

Remember, our goal is balance . . . always balance. Not either-or, but both-and. Not just *tough.* That, alone, makes a man cold, distant, intolerant, unbearable. But tough *and* tender . . . gentle, thoughtful, teachable, considerate.

Both.

Like Christ.

When Following Seems Unfair

They were sitting around a charcoal fire at the edge of the Sea of Galilee. Jesus and over half of His chosen disciples. It was dawn; quiet and cool. Smoke drifted lazily from the fire as well as the aroma of freshly toasted bread and smoked fish. Perhaps the fog hung low. No doubt small talk and a few laughs occurred as they breakfasted. Surely someone commented on how good it was to catch over 150 fish so *quickly.*

The sounds of these hungry men must have echoed across the placid waters of Galilee. How delightful it must have been to know they were reclining on the sand with the resurrected Savior in their midst.

Suddenly the conversation ceased. Jesus turned to Simon Peter. Their eyes met. For a few moments they talked together about the depth of Simon's love for his Lord. It must have been painful for the rough-hewn disciple, but he answered Jesus with honesty and humility.

Then, as abruptly as that conversation had begun, it ended—with a command. From Jesus to Peter. "Follow Me!" (John 21:19). Simple; easily understood; heard by everyone, especially Simon. The Lord wanted Simon's heart—without a single reservation. Jesus realized that His disciple was affectionately drawn to Him and greatly admired Him. But Jesus now told him to be totally available, fully committed with no strings attached. His command was perfectly calculated to get the fisherman off the fence.

Simon's response was classic. Verses 20 and 21 tell the story.

Peter, turning around, saw the disciple whom Jesus loved (John) *. . . and . . . seeing him said to Jesus, "Lord, and what about this man?"*

Isn't that typical? The finger was on Peter and he attempted to dodge

71

some of its pointed direction by asking Jesus about John. "What about John, Lord? You're asking me to follow you . . . how about *him?* Aren't you going to give him the same kind of command? After all, he's a disciple, too!"

Notice Jesus' reply in the very next verse. It must have stung.

Jesus said to him, "If I want him to remain until I come, what is that to you? You follow Me!"

This entire dialogue became permanently etched in Peter's memory. I am certain he *never* forgot the reproof.

Now what does this say to us—and what does it say to the members of our family? Simply this: Following Christ is an *individual* matter. The Lord saves us individually. He gifts and commissions us individually. He speaks to us and directs us individually. He maps our course and plots our path individually. Peter momentarily forgot this fact. He became overtly interested in the will of God for *John's* life.

Does that sound a little like you? It may be that God is putting you through an experience that seems terribly demanding, even humiliating. You are facing the rigors of an obedient walk . . . and you may be looking over the fence or across the dining room table, wondering about *his* life, or *her* commitment. You're entertaining the thought, "It simply is not fair."

"What is that to you?" asks Christ. When it comes to this matter of doing His will, God has not said that you must answer for anyone else except yourself. Quit looking around for equality! Stop concerning yourself with the need of others to do what you are doing. Or endure what you have been called to endure. God chooses the roles we play. Each part is unique.

Some couples seem uniquely allowed by God to endure hardship—the loss of a child, a lingering and crippling illness, financial bankruptcy, a fire that levels everything to ashes, an unexplainable series of tragedies. While others are hardly touched by difficulty. It's so very easy for the Peter within us to lash out and bitterly lobby for an Equal Wrongs Amendment before the Judge. His response remains the same: "You just follow Me, my child. Remember, you're not John . . . you're Peter."

Has God called you to a difficult or demanding mission field . . . or occupation . . . or type of ministry . . . or home situation? Has He led you to live sacrificially . . . or pass up a few pleasures? If He has—*follow Him!* And forget about *John,* okay? If Jesus is big enough to prod the *Peters,* then He is also big enough to judge the *Johns.*

Being Real

*D*ave Cowens, star basketball center for the Boston Celtics, disappeared. Without warning, he walked off the practice court, showered, dressed, and drove away. Alone.

He kept driving to . . . somewhere. His only explanation was the familiar comment, "I need to get my head together." He added that it could take as little as two weeks or as much as ten years. The sportscasters, management, team, spectators, and fans couldn't imagine what he was looking for.

I could.

The Carpenters do a number that helps explain the superstar's puzzling reaction. It's a peaceful soul-song that talks about needing a place to hide away . . . to be quiet . . . to think things through . . . to reflect.

Perhaps that's what the Boston superstar was trying to say. He's got everything imaginable—fame, possessions, job security, a strong body, lots of bucks—but maybe at that moment in his life he lacked something far more important. Something like a sense of purpose and inner fulfillment. Something which basketball and all its benefits could never provide. An inner itch that can't be scratched by achievement or people or things or activities. To scratch it requires a great deal of internal searching, which the athlete felt he couldn't do and still keep pace with the maddening NBA schedule.

To "find yourself" requires that you take time to look. It's essential if you want to be a whole person, real to the core.

Now I'm not advocating that one suddenly stop everything else so he can work the hide 'n' seek process. That's rather unrealistic even if you aren't the starting center for an NBA franchise. It's a little like remov-

ing an anthill in your backyard with six sticks of TNT. Or like setting your car on fire because the engine knocks. Learning to be whole isn't prompted by copping out. But there are times in all our lives when we need to back away, slow down, stay quiet, think through, be still.

"I'd rather burn out than rust out!" shouts the zealot. Frankly, neither sounds very appealing to me. Either way you're *out*. People who are burning out may start a lot of fires and stir up a lot of noise and smoke. But who cares—if everything turns to ashes? People who are rusting out may move about as slowly as a sloth and live to be 130. But so what—if all they accomplished in life is paying bills and staying out of jail?

There *has* to be more to life than just doing. There is! It's *being*. Becoming whole . . . believable . . . purposeful . . . lovable. The word is *real*. It takes time and it usually hurts.

The Velveteen Rabbit is a classy book for children with a message for adults. In it is a revealing nursery dialogue between a new toy rabbit and an old skin horse. As they are lying side by side one day, Rabbit asks Horse:

> *"What is REAL? Does it mean having things that buzz inside you and a stick-out handle?"*
>
> *"Real isn't how you are made,"* said the Skin Horse. *"It's a thing that happens to you. When a child loves you for a long, long time, not just to play with, but REALLY loves you, then you become REAL."*
>
> *"Does it hurt?"* asked the Rabbit.
>
> *"Sometimes,"* said the Skin Horse, for he was always truthful. *"When you are REAL you don't mind being hurt."*
>
> *"Does it happen all at once, like being wound up,"* he asked, *"or bit by bit?"*
>
> *"It doesn't happen all at once,"* said the Skin Horse. *"You become. It takes a long time. That's why it doesn't often happen to people who break easily, or have sharp edges, or have to be carefully kept. Generally, by the time you are Real, most of your hair has been loved off, and your eyes drop out and you get loose in the joints and very shabby. But these*

things don't matter at all, because once you are Real you can't be ugly, except to people who don't understand."[24]

Take a long look at *you,* suggests Skin Horse. Going through a lot of activities? Staying busy? In a hurry most of the time? Spinning around the squirrel cage? Seldom pausing to ask why? Still reluctant to be loved . . . to be real? Still keeping a distance between yourself and your family members? Still substituting *doing* for *being?*

It'll never satisfy. You cannot play cover-up forever. What does God suggest? Having a heart of compassion, being kind, tender, transparent, gentle, patient, forgiving, loving and lovable. All those things spell R-E-A-L.

I'm convinced that's what Cowens was looking for. He may not have found it in a few weeks, but it sure was worth the effort. Losing your hair takes time, and it's pretty painful to have your eyes drop out and your joints get loose. But in the long run, that's the only way to be.

REAL.

The Tongue of the Wise

Wisely labeled "the saving virtue," tact graces a life like fragrance graces a rose. One whiff of those red petals erases any memory of the thorns.

Tact is like that.

It's remarkable how peaceful and pleasant it can make us. Its major goal is avoiding unnecessary offense . . . and that alone ought to make us *crave* it. Its basic function is a keen sense of what to say or do in order to maintain the truth *and* good relationships . . . and that alone ought to make us *cultivate* it. Tact is *savoir faire* on the horizontal plane. It is incessantly appropriate, invariably attractive, incurably appealing, but rare . . . oh, so rare!

Remember the teacher you had who lacked tact? Learning was sacrificed daily on the altar of fear. You wondered each session if *that* was the day you'd be singled out and embarrassed through some public put-down.

Remember the salesman you encountered who lacked tact? Once you found out (and it usually doesn't take 60 seconds), you wanted only one thing—to get *away!*

Remember the boss you worked for who lacked tact? You never knew if he *ever* understood you or considered you to be a valuable person.

And who could forget that tactless physician? You weren't a human being, you were Case No. 36—a body with a blood pressure of 120/70 . . . height 5'7" . . . weight 160 . . . a chronic history of diarrhea . . . stones in your gall bladder—*"and you need radical surgery immediately!"* All this was spoken in perfect monotone as he glared grimly at a folder stuffed with X-rays, charts, and long sheets of paper covered with advanced hieroglyphics. Brilliant, capable, experienced, dignified, respected . . . but no tact.

Perhaps you heard about the husband who lacked tact. Early one morning his wife left for a trip abroad . . . and that very day their poodle died. When she called home that evening, she asked how everything was—and he bluntly blurted out, "Well, the dog died!" Shocked, she chided him through tears for being so tactless, so strong.

"What should I have said?" he asked.

"You should've broken the news gently, perhaps in stages. When I called you from here in New York, you could have said, 'The dog is on the roof.' And the next day when I called you from London, 'He fell off the roof.' The following day from Paris, you could have told me, 'He is at the vet's . . . in the hospital.' And finally, from Rome, I could have then been informed, 'He died.' ".

The husband paused and thought about the advice. His wife then asked, "By the way, how is mother?"

He responded, "She's on the roof!"

Ah, that's bad. But it isn't the worst. The classic example of tactless humanity, I'm disappointed to declare, is the abrasive Christian (so-called) who feels it is his or her calling to fight for the truth with little or no regard for the other fella's feelings. Of course, this is supposedly done in the name of the Lord. "To do anything less," this tactless individual intones with a pious expression, "would be compromise and counterfeit." So on he goes, plowing through people's feelings like a clumsy John Deere tractor, leaving them buried in the dirt and, worst of all, deeply offended. For all his rapid-fire Scripture quotations, you will rarely find Proverbs 18:19 on the lips of this armored crusader:

A brother offended is harder to be won than a strong city, and contentions are like the bars of a castle.

His favorite plan of attack is either to overlook or strongly demand, and the backwash is a back alley strewn with the litter of broken hearts and bitter souls. Unfortunately, the preacher himself is often the greatest offender, who seems to delight in developing a devastating

79

pulpit that scourges rather than encourages, that blasts rather than builds. His murder weapon is that blunt instrument hidden behind his teeth.

"The heart of the righteous ponders how to answer," wrote Solomon. That which turns away wrath is *"a gentle answer."*

The wise person uses his tongue to *"make knowledge acceptable,"* the king added. And who could ever forget the impact of the proverb that says: *"The tongue of the wise brings healing"* . . . or *"a man has joy in an apt answer and how delightful is a timely word!"*

There's a TV ad for a first-aid ointment that says, "Stop hurting . . . start healing." Another offers a bandage that takes the "ouch" away. That's good counsel. Let's be gentle and sensitive when we are touching the tender feelings of others. Moms and dads, it's hard to exaggerate the value of tact within the walls of your home. Soften the blows a little! You'll preserve some very valuable self-esteem while gaining respect, believe me.

By the way, no facts need be subtracted when tact is added. I used to sell shoes years ago. With a twinkle in his eye, my seasoned employer instructed me not to say, "Lady, your foot is too big for this shoe!" Instead, I was taught to say, "I'm sorry, ma'am, but this shoe is just a little too small for your foot." Both statements expressed the facts, but one was an insult and the other a tactful compliment. Same facts, different words.

It didn't shrink her foot, but it did save her face.

And that's what tact is all about.

Operation Relaxation

*S*ome days start right, others end right. This one did both, for a change. During the daylight hours things fell into place and as the evening approached, it got better! As planned, I got home before Monday Night Football. The smell of homemade clam chowder was lingering inside the front door. After hugging the kids and kissing the cook, I settled into my favorite chair . . . loosened my tie and kicked off my shoes. Detecting a new aroma, our miniature schnauzer, Heidi, moved across the room.

Upstairs, our two youngest were fiddling around with a rabbit, two hamsters, and a guinea pig—the protesting squeals of man and beast wafting down the stairwell. Our older daughter (finally off the phone) was out front enjoying the companionship of a neighbor gal . . . and a couple of guys, if I'm not mistaken. Curt was on the floor in his room strumming out a few chords on his steel strings—singing "Raindrops Keep Fallin' on My Head" as a lazy California sun was saying goodbye for the day. In between chopped onions and diced potatoes, Cynthia had doubled over with laughter as she tried to finish a chapter of Erma Bombeck's *The Grass is Always Greener Over the Septic Tank.*

No amount of money could buy the feeling that swept over me—incredible contentment . . . an inner sense of fulfillment . . . a surge of release and relief as the noise and pace of the world were strangely muffled by the sounds and smells of home. The comfortable fingers of nostalgia wrapped themselves around me and warmed me within.

Although my "to do" list was mostly "yet to be done," the day was over. Tomorrow would usher in its own sets of needs and responsibilities, but that was tomorrow. We all enjoyed supper (at half time, of course) then knocked out the cleanup in exactly five minutes . . . a new

Swindoll world record . . . as we moved faster than six speeding bullets, laughing like mad.

What therapy! How essential! And yet, how seldom families really relax. It's almost as though we're afraid to shift into neutral and let the motor idle. With a drive that borders near the neurotic, we Americans hit the floor running at 6 a.m. then drop, exhausted, at 12 midnight . . . scarcely able to remember what transpired during that 18-hour episode of relentless actions and words. If God is going to get our attention, He'd better plan on (1) making an appointment, (2) taking a number, or (3) pulling us over with a flashing red light on the freeway—otherwise, forget it! Strange, isn't it, that we place such a high priority on achievement we actually feel guilty when we accomplish nothing over a period of several hours. Such an experience requires justification when others ask, "What did you do last night?"

I visited a small town during a recent trip through central Oregon. It was one of those places that was so relaxed I found myself getting antsy. Life moves along there about the speed of a glacier. You know . . . the type of town where people gather to watch hub caps rust. I asked my friend:

"How do you stand it? Doesn't the slow pace drive you crazy?"

He responded with a smile. "Well, it took us about eight months to unwind. You gotta *learn* how to relax, Chuck. It isn't something that you do automatically. Now, we love it."

I've thought a lot about that. Relaxing isn't automatic. It's a skill that must be learned . . . cultivated. And since most of us don't live in a sleepy little town, here are a few suggestions to help you develop a workable plan.

1. Block out several evenings each month on your calendar. Make special plans to do *nothing*—except something you (or your family) would enjoy.

2. Loosen up the tight wires of your life by not taking yourself so seriously . . . nor your job. Sure, some things *are* terribly serious—but

not everything. The old Greek motto is still true: "You will break the bow if you keep it always bent."

3. Look for times during each day when something humorous or unusual makes laughter appropriate . . . then laugh out loud! That helps flush out the nervous system. Solomon tells us this is good medicine.

4. When you relax, *really relax* . . . blow it . . . enjoy the leisure . . . let out all the stops . . . ignore what some narrow-minded, squint-eyed critic might think or say. For sure, you'll get flack from those who rust out.

I'm of the opinion that a relaxed, easygoing Christian is miles more attractive and effective than the rigid, uptight brother who squeaks when he walks and whines when he talks.

Battle of the Bronze

It was the apostle John's final warning to his readers:

Little children, guard yourselves from idols (1 John 5:21).

"Watch out." says John. "Be on guard against anything that might occupy the place in your heart that should be reserved for God."

John never qualified that warning. The aged apostle deliberately refrained from classifying the idols or giving us a comprehensive list to follow. It's an unconditional command. *Any* idol, regardless of its beauty or usefulness or original purpose, is to be set aside so that Christ might reign supreme, without a single competitor.

I don't have many temptations to worship evil things. It's the *good* things that plague me. It isn't as difficult for me to reject something that is innately bad or wrong as it is to keep those good and wholesome things off the throne. That, I believe, is where the battle line begins.

Do you remember the experience of the Israelites in Numbers 21? They were hot and irritable as they wandered across the wilderness. They began to gripe about the lack of food and water. They complained again about the manna. So God sent snakes among them—"fiery serpents"—that bit many people and brought death into the camp. Realizing their sin, they begged Moses to ask God to remove the serpents. God told Moses to make a bronze serpent, hold it high upon a long pole . . . and whoever would look upon that bronze serpent would be healed. It wa a miraculous, glorious provision—and it worked. In fact, Jesus mentioned it in John 3:14-15 as an example of what He would accomplish when He died on a cross. The bronze serpent had been blessed of God and was, therefore, an effective means of deliverance.

But do you know what happened to that metalic snake? If you don't you're in for a big surprise. In 2 Kings 18:4 we read:

He (King Hezekiah) *removed the high places and broke down the sacred pillars and cut down the Asherah* (idol altars). *He also broke in pieces the bronze serpent that Moses had made, for until those days the sons of Israel burned incense to it; and it was called Nehushtan.*

This occurred about the sixth century B.C. The original event with the snakes took place much earlier—around 1450 B.C. For about *eight centuries* they had hung on to that bronze serpent. Can you believe that! They dragged it here and carried it there, preserved it, protected it, and polished it. Finally, they made an idol of it and even gave it a name: *Nehushtan.* That word simply means "a piece of bronze." And that's all it was. But they turned it into an object of worship. Something that had once been useful and effective had degenerated over the years into an idol.

It happens today. You can make an idol out of anything or anyone in life. A church building can become an idol to us, when all the while it is simply a place to meet and worship our Lord—nothing more. Your child can become your idol . . . in subtle ways you can so adore that little one that your whole life revolves around the child. Your mate or date can be given first place in your life and literally idolized. Your work can easily become your God . . . as can some pursuit in life. A house, a lawn, an antique, a car, a letter in sports, an education, a trip abroad, an achievement, and even that goal of "retirement" can so grip your heart that it becomes your Nehushtan.

Don't miss my point. There's nothing necessarily wrong with any of these good things. To possess them—any or all of them—is not sinful. But it is sinful when they *possess us!* Therein lies the difference. It's that sort of thing that turns a golden dream into a hollow chunk of bronze.

Honestly now . . . can you testify to the fact that you've destroyed the idols? Can you really say you are free from bronze anchors? That Christ reigns without a rival? Or would you have to admit to a personal shrine in your inner temple where you privately burn incense?

"Where your treasure is," says the Lord, "your heart is," and, "out of the abundance of your heart, your mouth speaks." What does that actually mean? What you invest your time and treasure in, what you talk about, what you keep returning to in your mind reveals what's really on your heart. It's just that simple.

Your Lord and Savior wants to occupy first place. Matthew 6:33 says that when He *has* it, everything else will be added to you. How long has it been since you've enlisted your Lord's help in a private, personal temple-cleansing session? It's so easy to get attached to idols. Good things, inappropriately adored. But when you have Jesus in the center of the room, everything else only junks up the decor.

He is also head of the body, the church; and He is the beginning, the first-born from the dead; so that He Himself might come to have first place in everything (Colossians 1:18).

Did you get that? First place in everything.
Everything.

Houdini's Secret

*E*hrich Weiss was a remarkable man.

By the time of his death he was famous around the world.

Never heard of him, huh?

Maybe this will help. He was born of Hungarian-Jewish parentage at Appleton, Wisconsin, in 1894. He became the highest paid entertainer of his day.

That still doesn't help much, does it? This will.

When he finally got his act together, Weiss adopted a stage name: *Harry Houdini.* The master showman, a distinguished flyer, a mystifying magician, and—most of all—an unsurpassed escapologist.

On March 10, 1904, the London *Daily Illustrated Mirror* challenged Houdini to escape from a special pair of handcuffs they had prepared. Are you ready? There were six locks on each cuff and nine tumblers on each lock! Seven days later, 4,000 spectators gathered in the London Hippodrome to witness the outcome of the audacious challenge which Houdini had accepted.

At precisely 3:15 p.m., the manacled showman stepped into an empty cabinet which came up to his waist. Kneeling down, he was out of sight for a full 20 minutes. He stood up smiling as the crowd applauded, thinking he was free. But he was not. He asked for more light. They came on brighter as he knelt down out of sight. Fifteen minutes later he stood to his feet. Applause broke out—again, premature. He was still handcuffed. Said he just needed to flex his knees.

Down into the cabinet again went the magician. Twenty minutes passed slowly for the murmuring crowd before Houdini stood to his feet with a broad smile. Loud applause quickly stopped as the audience saw he was not yet free. Because the bright lights made the heat so intense, he leaped from the cabinet and twisted his manacled hands in front of him until he could reach a pocket knife in his vest. Opening the knife with his teeth, he held its handle in his mouth and bent forward to such a degree that the tail of his coat fell over his head. He grasped the coat, pulled it over his head, then proceeded to slash it to ribbons with the knife between his teeth. Throwing aside the strips of his heavy coat, he jumped back into the box as the audience roared its approval and cheered him on.

Down went Houdini, but this time for only ten minutes. With a dramatic flourish, he jumped from the box—wrists free—waving the bulky handcuffs over his head in triumph. Pandemonium exploded in London! Once again the showman had achieved the incredible—almost the *impossible.*

Afterwards, Houdini was interviewed. Everyone wanted to know why he had to interrupt the process of his escape as often as he did. With a twinkle in his eyes, the magician freely admitted that he really didn't *have* to interrupt the process. He repeatedly explained that his ability to escape was based on knowledge.

"My brain is the key that sets me free!" he often declared. Then why did he keep standing up before he was loose? He confessed it was because he wanted the audience's applause to keep up his enthusiasm![25]

Two things, then set Houdini free: (1) his *knowledge* of what he knew to be true and (2) the cultivation of his own *enthusiasm.*

What an essential role enthusiasm plays in our lives! In many ways, it is the key ingredient that frees us from the cramping, dark, overheated confinement of a task. When the odds are against us, the hours are long, and the end is not yet in view, enthusiasm rescues us from the temptation to quit—or run away—or complain. It takes the grit and grind out of boredom. It calls in fresh troops when the battle gets long and the body gets weary.

Athletes feed on it. Salesmen are motivated by it. Teachers count on it. Students fail without it. Leadership demands it. Projects are completed because of it. Emerson's motto is as true today as the day he wrote it:

Nothing great was ever achieved without enthusiasm.[26]

Few characteristics are more contagious, more magnetic. I'm convinced that one of the reasons God gives us so many personal promises in His Word is to stir up our enthusiasm—to build a bonfire in the steamroom of our souls.

Houdini had it right: Knowledge is essential—but knowledge without enthusiasm is like a tire without air . . . like a pool without water . . . like a bed without sheets . . . like a "thank you" without a smile. Remove enthusiasm from a church service on Sunday and you have the makings of a memorial service at a mortuary on a Monday. Remove enthusiasm from the daily whirl of family activities and you've made a grinding mill out of a merry-go-round. Enthusiasm acts as the oil on Saturdays in our home when it's clean-up day and the family machine needs a boost.

Two men were in a military prison. One was sad and depressed. The other was quite happy. The sad soldier lamented that he had gone AWOL and was in for 30 days. His smiling companion replied that he had murdered a general and was in for 3 days. Astonished, the gloomy GI complained, "That isn't fair! Your crime was far more serious. Why am I in for 30 days—and you for only three?" Still smiling, the other answered, "They're going to hang me on Wednesday."[27]

The difference? Enthusiasm.

Songless Saints

I was on a scriptural safari. Prowling through the Ephesian letter, I was tracking an elusive, totally unrelated verse when God's sharp sword flashed, suddenly slicing me to the core.

speaking to one another in psalms and hymns and spiritual songs, singing and making melody with your heart to the Lord (Ephesians 5:19).

Everyone knows Ephesians 5:<u>18</u>, where we are told to "be filled with the Spirit" . . . but have you ever noticed that verse 18 ends with a comma, not a period? The next verse describes the very first result of being under the Spirit's control . . . *we sing!* We make melody with our hearts. We communicate His presence within us by presenting our own, individual concert of sacred music to Him.

Let's take it another step. The church building is not once referred to in Ephesians 5. I mention that because we Christians have so centralized our singing that we seldom engage in it once we drive away from the building with stained glass and an organ. Stop and think. Did you sing on the way *home* from church last Sunday? How about Monday, when you drove to work . . . or around the supper table . . . or Tuesday as you dressed for the day? Chances are, you didn't even sing before or after you spent some time with the Lord *any* day last week.

Why? The Spirit-filled saint is a song-filled saint! Animals can't sing. Neither can pews or pulpits or Bibles or buildings. Only you. And your melody is broadcast right into heaven —live—where God's antenna is always receptive . . . where the soothing strains of your song are always appreciated.

Believe me, if Martin Luther lived today, he'd be heartsick. That rugged warrior of the faith had two basic objectives when he fired the reformation cannon into the 16th-century wall of spiritual ignorance. First, he wanted to give the people a Bible they could read on their own, and second, to give them a hymnal so they could sing on their own. The Bible we have, and its words we read. The hymnal we have, but where, oh, where has the melody gone? Mr. Songless Saint is about as acquainted with his hymnal as his six-year-old daughter is with the Dow Jones averages. Christians know more verses by heart from Ecclesiastes and Ezekiel than from the well-worn hymnal they use over 100 times a year! We simply do not sing as often as we ought, and therein lies the blame and the shame.

Allow me to offer a few corrective suggestions:

Whenever and wherever you sing, concentrate on the words. If it helps, close your eyes. Let yourself get so lost in the accompanying melody that you momentarily forget where you are and what others might think. Frankly, I find it impossible to praise my Lord in song at the same time I feel self-conscious.

Make a concentrated effort to add one or two songs to your day. Remind yourself periodically of the words of a chorus or hymn you love and add them to your driving schedule or soap-and-shower time.

Sing often with a friend or members of your family. It helps melt down all sorts of invisible barriers. Singing before grace at mealtime in the evening is *so* enjoyable, but I warn you, you may become addicted.

Blow the dust off your record player and put on some beautiful music in the house. The family atmosphere will change for the better if you do this occasionally. And don't forget to sing along, adding your own harmony and "special" effects.

Never mind how beautiful or pitiful you may sound. Sing loud enough to drown out those defeating thoughts that normally clamor for attention. Release yourself from that cage of introspective reluctance—SING OUT! You are not auditioning for the choir, you're making melody with your heart.

If you listen closely when you're through, you may hear the hosts of heaven shouting for joy. Then again, it might be your neighbor . . . screaming for relief.

93

Monuments

Not far from Lincoln, Kansas, stands a strange group of gravestones. A guy named Davis, a farmer and self-made man, had them erected. He began as a lowly hired hand and by sheer determination and frugality he managed to amass a considerable fortune in his lifetime. In the process, however, the farmer did not make many friends. Nor was he close to his wife's family, since they thought she had married beneath her dignity. Embittered, he vowed never to leave his in-laws a thin dime.

When his wife died, Davis erected an elaborate statue in her memory. He hired a sculptor to design a monument which showed both her and him at opposite ends of a love seat. He was so pleased with the result that he commissioned another statue—this time of himself, kneeling at her grave, placing a wreath on it. That impressed him so greatly that he planned a third monument, this time of his wife keeling at *his* future gravesite, depositing a wreath. He had the sculptor add a pair of wings on her back, since she was no longer alive, giving her the appearance of an angel. One idea led to another until he'd spent no less than a quarter million dollars on the monuments to himself and his wife!

Whenever someone from the town would suggest he might be interested in a community project (a hospital, a park and swimming pool for the children, a municipal building, etc.), the old miser would frown, set his jaw and shout back, "What's this town ever done for me? I don't owe this town nothin'!"

After using up all his resources on stone statues and selfish pursuits, John Davis died at 92, a grim-faced resident of the poorhouse. But the monuments . . . it's strange . . . . Each one is slowly sinking into the Kansas soil, fast becoming victims of time, vandalism, and neglect.

Monuments of spite. Sad reminders of a self-centered, unsympathetic life. There is a certain poetic justice in the fact that within a few years, they will all be gone.

Oh, by the way, very few people attended Mr. Davis' funeral. It is reported that only one person seemed genuinely moved by any sense of personal loss. He was Horace England . . . the tombstone salesman.[28]

Before we're too severe with the late Mr. Davis, let's take an honest look at the monuments being erected today—some of which are no less revealing, if not quite so obvious. A close investigation will reveal at least four:

- FORTUNE
- FAME
- POWER
- PLEASURE

Much the same as the Davis gravestone, these monuments are built in clusters, making them appear formidable . . . and acceptable. As the idols in ancient Athens, our society is saturated with them.

FORTUNE. How neatly it fits our times! Its inscription at the base is bold: "Get rich." The statuesque figures in the monument are impressive: a hard-working young executive; a clever, diligent businessman unwilling to admit to the greed behind his long hours and relentless drive.

FAME. Another monument tailor-made for Century Twenty. It reads: "Be famous." All its figures are bowing in worship to the popularity cult; eagerly anticipating the day when their desire to be known, seen, quoted, applauded and exalted will be satisfied. Young and old surround the scene.

POWER. Etched in the flesh of this human edifice are the words: "Take control." These figures are capitalizing on every opportunity to seize the reins of authority and race to the top . . . regardless. "Look out for number one!"

PLEASURE. The fourth monument is perhaps the most familiar of all. Its message, echoed countless times in the media, is straightforward: "Indulge yourself." If it looks good, enjoy it! If it tastes good, drink it! If it feels good, do it! Like the line out of the Academy Award winning song "You Light Up My Life" that says:

It can't be wrong
If it feels so right . . . .

Conspicuous by its absence is the forgotten philosophy of Jesus Christ. He's the One who taught the truth about being eternally rich through giving rather than getting. About serving others rather than leaving footprints on their back in the race for the farthest start. About surrendering rights rather than clamoring for more control. About limiting your liberty out of love and saying "No" when the flesh pleads for "Yes." You know—the whole package wrapped up in one simple statement . . .

. . . seek first His kingdom, and His righteousness; and all these things shall be added to you (Matthew 6:33).

No elaborate set of statues. No sculptures done in marble—not even an epitaph for the world to read. And when He died, few cared because few understood. They were too busy building their own monuments.

We still are.

Back Home

Of all life's pressures, none is harder to bear than trouble at home. Financial pressure is tough, but not impossible to work through. Physical pain is bad—sometimes *horrible*—but usually not without hope. The loss of a job or failure at school may bring to the surface feelings of desperation, but this too will pass.

There is, however, nothing to compare with the lingering, agonizing, tortuous heartache brought on by a rebellious and wayward child. Too big to spank. Too angry to reason with. Too volatile to threaten. Too stubborn to warn. Determined to run free of authority . . . regardless. The rebel has one great desire in life (borrowing from Sinatra's hit)—to say:

"I did it *my* way."

Maddened with an adventurous lust for excitement, anxious to burst from the tight cocoon of parental control, the young anarchist creates havoc in a home before finally deciding to fly wild and free. Soon it occurs. With the slam of a door. "I'm gone forever!"

At that moment, both sides feel a measure of bitter-sweet relief. But not for long. At home, peace returns. Along with silence. Which mates with memories. Bearing crippled offspring: guilt, grief, shame.

A foolish son is a grief to his father
And bitterness to her who bore him (Proverbs 17:25).

If you have been there, no one needs to elucidate. The brokenhearted mom and dad need a comforter, not a commentator. It is agony at its highest peak. Imagination, like the rebel, runs wild, as worry, fear, and empathy play mental music in a minor key.

Time crawls. No word. The chill of winter and the rains of spring merely widen the chasm of silence. No word. Summer's furnace and fall's colors do little to temper the edge of parental anxiety. No word.

Prayer becomes a lonely vigil. At times, the empty, hopeless repetition of sounds struggling out of a swollen face. Thoughts are confused. And endless.

Where did we go wrong . . .?
Will we ever see each other again . . .?
Is he/she safe . . .?
If we had it to do over again . . . .
How did it all start . . .?
Should we . . . could we . . .?

Still, no word.

Winter returns, but not the wayward. The icy blast pushes its way through windows and doors, but the phone doesn't ring and a knock doesn't come. No familiar voice breaks the silence.

And then. Unannounced. Suddenly. At the least expected moment, the prodigal comes back . . . back to where life makes up its mind. Home.

A lean profile can be seen on the horizon. Shoulders are stooped. Head bowed. Long lines of remorse, disgrace, humiliation stretch across that once-defiant face. Wasted and repentant, with only a few soft-spoken whispers of apology . . . the wayward one slumps into the arms of the waiting dad. As time momentarily stops. And two hearts beat together again. One forgiving, the other forgiven.

And God smiles.

It happens everyday.

Someday

$\mathcal{S}$OMEDAY WHEN THE KIDS ARE GROWN, things are going to be a lot different. The garage won't be full of bikes, electric train tracks on plywood, sawhorses surrounded by chunks of two-by-fours, nails, a hammer and saw, unfinished "experimental projects," and the rabbit cage. I'll be able to park both cars neatly in just the right places, and never again stumble over skateboards, a pile of papers (saved for the school fund drive), or the bag of rabbit food—now split and spilled. Ugh!

SOMEDAY WHEN THE KIDS ARE GROWN, the kitchen will be incredibly neat. The sink will stay free of sticky dishes, the garbage disposal won't get choked on rubber bands or paper cups, the refrigerator won't be clogged with nine bottles of milk, and we won't lose the tops to jelly jars, catsup bottles, the peanut butter, the margarine, or the mustard. The water jar won't be put back empty, the ice trays won't be left out overnight, the blender won't stand for six hours coated with the remains of a midnight malt, and the honey will stay *inside* the container.

SOMEDAY WHEN THE KIDS ARE GROWN, my lovely wife will actually have time to get dressed leisurely. A long hot bath (without three panic interruptions), time to do her nails (even toenails if she pleases!) without answering a dozen questions and reviewing spelling words, having had her hair done that afternoon without trying to squeeze it in between racing a sick dog to the vet and a trip to the orthodontist with a kid in a bad mood because she lost her headgear.

SOMEDAY WHEN THE KIDS ARE GROWN, the instrument called a "telephone" will actually be available. It won't look like it's growing from a teenager's ear. It will simply hang there . . . silently and amazingly available! It will be free of lipstick, human saliva, mayonaise, corn chip crumbs, and toothpicks stuck in those little holes.

SOMEDAY WHEN THE KIDS ARE GROWN, I'll be able to see *through* the car windows. Fingerprints, tongue licks, sneaker footprints, and dog tracks (nobody knows how) will be conspicuous by their absence. The back seat won't be a disaster area, we won't sit on jacks or crayons any more, the tank will not always be somewhere between empty and fumes and (glory to God!) I won't have to clean up dog messes another time.

SOMEDAY WHEN THE KIDS ARE GROWN, we will return to normal conversations. You know, just plain American talk. "Gross" won't punctuate every sentence seven times. "Yuk!" will not be heard. "Hurry up, I gotta go!" will not accompany the banging of fists on the bathroom door. "It's my turn" won't call for a referee. And a magazine article will be read in full without interruption, then discussed at length without mom and dad having to hide in the attic to finish the conversation.

SOMEDAY WHEN THE KIDS ARE GROWN, we won't run out of toilet tissue. My wife won't lose her keys. We won't forget to shut the refrigerator door. I won't have to dream up new ways of diverting attention from the gumball machine . . . or have to answer "Daddy, is it a sin that you're driving 47 in a 30-mile-an-hour zone?" . . . or promise to kiss the rabbit goodnight . . . or wait up forever until they get home from dates . . . or have to take a number to get a word in at the supper table . . . or endure the pious pounding of one Keith Green just below the level of acute pain.

YES, SOMEDAY WHEN THE KIDS ARE GROWN, things are going to be a lot different. One by one they'll leave our nest, and the place will begin to resemble order and maybe even a touch of elegance. The clink of china and silver will be heard on occasion. The crackling of the fireplaces will echo through the hallway. The phone will be strangely silent. The house will be

quiet . . .

and calm . . .

and always clean . . .

and empty . . .

and filled with memories . . .

and lonely . . .

and we won't like that at all. And we'll spend our time not looking forward to *Someday* but looking back to *Yesterday.* And thinking, "Maybe we can baby-sit the grandkids and get some *life* back in this place for a change!"

Could it be that the apostle Paul had some of this in mind when he wrote:

. . . I have learned to be content in whatever circumstances I am (Philippians 4:11).

Maybe so. But then again, chances are good Paul never had to clean up many dog messes.

Footnotes:

[1] Gordon MacDonald, *The Effective Father* (Wheaton: Tyndale House Publishers, 1977), pp. 13-14.

[2] Edith Schaeffer, *What Is a Family?* (Old Tappan, New Jersey: Fleming H. Revell Company, 1975), p. 119.

[3] Jerry White, *Honesty, Morality, and Conscience* (Colorado Springs, Colorado: NavPress, 1978), p. 49.

[4] J. Oswald Sanders, *Spiritual Leadership* (Chicago: Moody Press, 1967), pp. 59-60. Used by permission.

[5] Sanders, p. 60.

[6] Alfred Lord Tennyson, *Familiar Quotations,* ed. John Bartlett (Boston: Little, Brown and Company, 1955), p. 550a.

[7] *The Joy of Words* (Chicago: J.G. Ferguson Publishing Co., 1960), p. 89.

[8] Bruce Larson, *The One and Only You* (Waco, Texas: Word Books, 1974), pp. 84-85. Adaptation by permission of Word Books, Publisher, Waco, Texas 76703.

[9] B.J. Thomas, "Home Where I Belong" Words and music by Pat Terry, copyright 1976 by Word Music, Inc. All Rights Reserved. International Copyright Secured. Used by permission.

[10] Leslie B. Flynn, *Great Church Fights* (Wheaton: Victor Books, 1976), p. 105.

[11] Flynn, p. 104.

[12] Flynn, p. 105.

[13] Sir William Osler, *Familiar Quotations,* ed. John Bartlett (Boston: Little, Brown and Company, 1955), p. 744b.

[14] C.S. Lewis, *Screwtape Letters* (New York: Macmillan Publishing Co., Inc., 1942), p. 62.

[15] Lewis, p. 124.

[16] Hazel Werner, *Quote Unquote,* ed. Lloyd Cory (Wheaton: Victor Books, 1977), p. 154.

[17] Socrates, *Familiar Quotations,* ed. John Bartlett (Boston: Little, Brown and Company, 1955), p. 20b.

[18] *Inside the Ark Learning Center* and "What's Going on Here," Springfield, Oregon Public Schools Newsletter, Vol. 1, No. 8, Feb. 8, 1975.

[19] William Shakespeare, *Familiar Quotations,* ed. John Bartlett (Boston: Little, Brown and Company, 1955), p. 191a.

[20] Paul Tournier, *To Understand Each Other* (Atlanta: John Knox Press, ©1967 by M.E. Bratcher), p.8.

[21] Paul Simon, "Sounds of Silence," ©1964, 1965 Paul Simon. Used by permission.

[22] Samuel Butler, "The Act of Listening," *The Royal Bank of Canada Monthly Letter,* Vol. 60, No. 1, January 1979, p. 2.

[23] Joyce Landorf, *Tough and Tender* (Old Tappan, New Jersey: Fleming H. Revell Company, 1975), p. 156.

[24] Margery Williams, *The Velveteen Rabbit* (New York: Doubleday and Company, Inc., 1958), pp. 16-17. Reprinted by permission.

[25] Bruce W. Thielemann, *There is a Way Out* (Glendale, California: Gospel Light Publications [Regal Book], 1975), pp. 39-43.

[26] Ralph Waldo Emerson, *Familiar Quotations,* ed. John Bartlett (Boston: Little, Brown and Company, 1955), p. 502b.

[27] Thielemann, p. 39.

[28] Charles L. Allen, *You Are Never Alone* (Old Tappan, New Jersey: Fleming H. Revell Company 1978), pp. 145-146.